Diaspora
and
Nation-Building

Diaspora and Nation-Building

Editors
Dr. Ruchi Verma
Dr. Nutan Pandey
Shri Narayan Kumar
Amb. Anup K. Mudgal

PRABHAT PRAKASHAN
prabhatbooks@gmail.com

Antar Rashtriya Sahayog Parishad
arspindia@gmail.com

Published by
PRABHAT PRAKASHAN
4/19 Asaf Ali Road,
New Delhi-110 002 (INDIA)
Tele : +91-11-23289777
e-mail: prabhatbooks@gmail.com

ISBN 978-93-5322-847-7
DIASPORA AND NATION-BUILDING
Edited by Dr. Ruchi Verma, Dr. Nutan Pandey,
Shri Narayan Kumar, Amb. Anup K. Mudgal

Edition
First, 2019

© Reserved

Preface

Antar Rashtriya Sahyog Parishad (ARSP), New Delhi organised a two-day International Conference in Mauritius on 5-6 July, 2018 on the topic: 'Contribution of Diaspora in Nation Building' in partnership with the Aapravasi Ghat Trust Fund (AGTF) and Mahatma Gandhi Institute (MGI) from Mauritius. The conference was organised in continuation of the ARSP's year-long commemoration of the centenary of the abolition of the Indentured system and as a part of the celebrations to mark the fiftieth anniversary year of the Mauritian independence.

The Conference discussed the role of diaspora in nation-building, providing a comprehensive perspective from the history to the contemporary developments in political, economic and socio-cultural fields as also their future vision. Besides the formal opening and closing sessions, there were six technical sessions to develop various themes. The Conference attracted senior level participation from Mauritius, other countries of the so-called 'Indentured Route' and India.

The Rt. Hon. Sir Anerood Jugnauth, former Prime Minister and currently Minister Mentor graced the opening session as the Chief Guest and formally inaugurated the conference on 5 July morning. The opening session was also addressed by Minister of Culture, Mr. Prithvirajsing Roopun, Chairman MGI Mr. Jaynarain Meetoo, and Chairman AGTF, Mr. Dharam Yash Deo Dhuny. From the ARSP, their President and Secretary General welcomed the participating dignitaries, scholars and experts, and also briefed them about the contribution of ARSP in promoting the interests and role of diaspora in the wholesome development of their relations with India.

The closing session was presided over by the acting President, HE Paramasivum Pillay Vyapoory, on 6 July afternoon. The session was also addressed by Minister of Tourism, Mr. Anil Kumarsingh Gayan and DG, MGI Dr. Sooryakanti Narsimloo Gayan.

Today, there are over thirty three million members of Indian diaspora, settled in over hundred countries. Given their hardworking nature and liberal values of democracy, open-mindedness, tolerance, accommodation and affinity for peace, they have not only assimilated as inseparable members of their adopted societies but have excelled in fields of education, technology and business. In many countries, the diaspora is making valuable contributions to the development process. They are widely respected as the drivers of cutting edge technology, skills and more recently as prominent investors and generators of wealth, prosperity and jobs.

In keeping with their all-round and constructive contributions to their adopted countries, the diaspora members have also been expanding their footprints into the field of local politics. In a conference of diaspora Parliamentarians organised by the Ministry of External Affairs in New Delhi last year, over 140 PIO Parliamentarians and Mayors attended from 23 countries. The ARSP had the unique privilege of hosting a day-long interactive conference with the participants. The event was presided over by the Honourable President of India.

The diaspora is also making important contribution to the development in India by way of remittances, technology transfer and skills. They are also an important bridge connecting India and their adopted countries, thereby strengthening global trust and goodwill for India.

An important and special constituent of the Indian diaspora has been the countries of the so-called Indentured Route, where millions of Indian workers were taken by the colonial powers under the Indentured system for addressing labour shortages in their plantations following the abolition of slavery. Over two million Indian workers were taken to far off lands in Africa (Mauritius, South Africa), the Caribbean (Trinidad and Tobago, Surinam, Guyana) and Pacific (Fiji). In many of these lands, the descendants of the Indentured Indian workers constituted significant majorities and played important role not only in the liberation movements of these countries, but subsequent nation-building process. Besides occupying important political and constitutional positions, they have made immense contribution to the overall socio-economic development of their respective countries. They have also played a significant role in the preservation of their Indian cultural values and active contacts with their roots. All these countries and societies have a special place in India's outreach for diaspora, including development partnership.

ARSP has a long history of working very closely with the countries of the so-called 'Indentured Route' and organised year-long activities to commemorate the centenary of the abolition of the Indentured system during 2017-18. In continuation of this initiative and to mark the 50th Anniversary year of the Independence of Mauritius, the ARSP, with the support of Ministry of External Affairs, organised this international conference on the 'CONTRIBUTION OF DIASPORA IN NATION-BUILDING'.

Besides the opening and the valedictory functions, the Conference had a total of six technical sessions, devoted to discussion on the contributions of diaspora in the areas of: i) independence movements and political developments setting the stage and practices of modern democracy, including the establishment and growth of democratic institutions; ii) economic development and modernisation; iii) socio-cultural development including technology and higher education; iv) diaspora and nation-building – Mauritius, a case study, and v) an open house for discussion on any subject of interest.

The Conference in Mauritius was followed by a day-long worship with all diaspora organisations in Reunion on 6 July.

8

Over 75 leaders from prominent Indian diaspora organisations attended the workshop and participated in lively discussion. This was perhaps the first such wide scale interaction with the Indian diaspora in the Reunion.

Presentations by the experts were followed by very rich discussion in all sessions and this book primarily captures the essence of these deliberations. We hope this publication would be a useful resource for researchers in the fields of migration and diaspora studies.

Finally, I would like to place on record our sincere gratitude to all our partners and participants, particularly HE Paramasivum Pillay Vyapoory, the President of Mauritius; The Rt. Hon. Sir Anerood Jugnauth, Former Prime Minister and Minister Mentor; Hon. Mr. Prithvirajsing Roopun; Mr. Anil Kumarsingh Gayan; Mr. Jaynarain Meetoo; Mr. Dharam Yash Deo Dhuny; and Mrs. Sooryakanti Narsimloo Gayan for their guidance and support. I sincerely thank the Ministry of External Affairs, Government of India for all their support. I would also like to offer my sincere gratitude to Sh. Abhay Thakur, High Commissioner of India in Mauritius and his team, and Sh. Babu Paul, Consul General of India in Reunion and his Team for their excellent arrangements and support for making these events a great success. Lastly, the Editorial team has done an excellent job and they deserve our whole-hearted appreciation.

—**Amb. Virendra Gupta,**
President, ARSP,
New Delhi.

Contents

Preface	*5*
1. The Aapravasi Ghat Trust Fund (AGTF)	11
2. Mahatma Gandhi Institute (MGI)	13
3. Antar Rashtriya Sahayog Parishad (ARSP)	16
4. Aapravasi Ghat : A Memorial of our Indian Ancestors' Sufferings	18
5. The Tradition of Hardwork, Tolerance and Resilience	21
6. The Rise and Growth of Indians as a Political Force in Mauritius and Fiji: A Comparative Overview	26
7. Strengthening India's Strategic Engagement with Indo-Caribbean Diaspora	36
8. Social and Political Participation of Indian Diaspora in the UK	62
9. Critical Challenges the Indian Diaspora Must Confront	71
10. Diaspora and Sustainable Economic Development	74
11. Roles of Mauritian Expatriates in the Promotion of Nation-building through Bhojpuri Patriotic Songs	85
12. The Role of the Indian Diasporic Intangible Heritage in Identity Creation and Nation-Building in Mauritius	96

13. The Role of the Arts/Performing Arts in the Socio-cultural Practice of Indian Indentured Immigrants: Towards Nation Building in Mauritius — 103

14. Diaspora and Nation-Building: An Indo-Mauritian Perspective — 110

15. Indian Diaspora and Culture on the French Territory Reunion — 129

16. Indian Diaspora: Contribution of Diaspora in Nation-Building — 137

17. Role of Indian Diaspora in Nation-Building: The Mauritian Experience — 149

18. The Contribution of Women Towards Nation-Building in Mauritius: A Qualitative Study — 165

19. Closing Statement by D.G, MGI & RTI — 177

20. Statement by Hon. Minister of Tourism, Republic of Mauritius — 181

21. Statement by H.E The President, Republic of Mauritius — 186

22. Vote of Thanks — 190

23. Summary Report of the Conference (Mauritius) — 193

24. Summary Report of the Conference (Re-Union) — 200

About the Contributors/Authors — *206*

The Aapravasi Ghat Trust Fund (AGTF)

Mission and Vision

The Aapravasi Ghat Trust Fund, AGTF is a body corporate under the aegis of the Ministry of Arts and Culture. It was created in 2001 by the Government of the Republic of Mauritius through Act of Parliament to manage and promote the Aapravasi Ghat Site. The site was declared National Monument under the National Monuments Act in 1987 (GN31/87) and subsequently proclaimed National Heritage in 2003 under the National Heritage Act, 2003.

Vision

The Trust's guiding principles include:

- To support activities related to Indentured Labour immigration.
- To support projects that benefit all Mauritians and in which Mauritians from all walks of life can participate. This includes the conceptualisation, planning and execution of projects.
- To restore the links with the past and our origins those have been broken as a result of rapid modernisation and to restore pride for our Indenture Heritage.
- To carry our projects in a democratic spirit, in a historically accurate way and in full respect of the multi-cultural society in which we live.
- To promote excellence rather than be satisfied with the basic minimum or the cheapest alternative.

Mission

The AGTF was entrusted to:

- Establish and promote the Aapravasi Ghat as a national, regional and international memorial site;
- Preserve and restore the aesthetic and architectural aspects of the Aapravasi Ghat;
- Set up a museum at Aapravasi Ghat and create public awareness of the history of the site;
- Promote social and cultural aspects of the Aapravasi Ghat;
- Encourage and support projects and publications related to the Indentured labour system;
- Establish links with appropriate national, regional and international organisations; and
- Identify and acquire sites, buildings and structures linked with the history of the arrival of immigrants in Mauritius.

☐

Mahatma Gandhi Institute (MGI)

The Mahatma Gandhi Institute (MGI) is an apex institute of oriental learning of the Government of Mauritius established with the support of the Government of India. The foundation stone of the Institute was laid on June 3, 1970 by Smt. Indira Gandhi and it was inaugurated on October 9, 1976 jointly by Sir Seewoosagur Ramgoolam and Smt. Indira Gandhi, the then Prime Ministers of Mauritius and India. Its

14 *Diaspora and Nation-Building*

mission is to provide academic and cultural basis for the promotion, consolidation and dissemination of Indian cultural traditions within the multicultural context of Mauritius. The Institute has a mandate to promote Indian Studies, Performing Arts, Fine Arts, Mauritian Studies, Chinese Studies and African Studies. The High Commissioner of India is the ex-officio Vice-chairperson of the Council of the Institute, which is headed by a Chairperson nominated by the Government of Mauritius.

MGI runs a network of five secondary schools located in various regions of the country and one Form Six College (Senior Secondary School) as well as the Gandhian Basic School, which specialises in pre-vocational education based on Gandhian principles. This school provides vocational training to the dropouts at primary level.

The MGI has the responsibility of maintaining the archives of Indian immigrants to Mauritius. The archives are well maintained and are an authentic repository of the arrival records of the Indian indentured labourers from 1834. This information is used as an authentic document for the issuance of Person of Indian Origin (PIO) cards.

In October 1998, a one-time grant of Indian ` 50 lakhs and a recurring annual grant of ` 5 lakhs for a period of 10 years was approved for the MGI. The grant has been released through the Central Institute of Indian Languages (CIIL), Mysore for collaborative activities under an MOU signed between MGI and CIIL on April 28, 2005.

The Jawaharlal Nehru Chair for Indian Studies was established at MGI in 1993 for a period of 10 years with the support of Government of India. The Chair was administered under the Indian Technical and Economic Co-operation (ITEC) scheme from 1999 to 2003.

The Institute has brought Indian studies, especially Indian languages, philosophy and culture into the mainstream of the Mauritian education. Through its education facilities, the School of Mauritian, Asian and African studies, Folklore

Museum, Fine Arts building, Gandhian Basic School for crafts learning and a rich library, the Institute has served as a bridge for bringing together the cultures of the two countries and has enriched the understanding of each other.

Each year on October 2, Mahatma Gandhi's birthday, the MGI organises the Gandhi Memorial Lecture, delivered by a distinguished personality.

□

Antar Rashtriya Sahayog Parishad (ARSP)

Antar Rashtriya Sahayog Parishad-Bharat (ARSP) was established in 1978 by public spirited eminent personalities who were pioneers in their fields. It is a non-profit, non-governmental and non-political organisation devoted to promoting universal brotherhood and harmony, embodied in its motto, 'Vasudhaiva Kutumbakam' (The Whole World is One Family). In furtherance of its charter, ARSP pays special attention to the Indian Diaspora. From the very beginning,

Antar Rashtriya Sahayog Parishad (ARSP)   17

ARSP was led by illustrious and eminent personalities like Dr. Dharma Vira (former Governor of West Bengal), Shri Bhagwan Singh (former High Commissioner of India to Fiji), Dr. Sarojini Mahishi (former Minister of State, Government of India), Shri Lakhan Lal Mehrotra (former Secretary, Ministry of External Affairs), Shri Ved Prakash Goyal (former Cabinet Minister) and Amb. Shashank (former Foreign Secretary). Veteran Journalist and Social Activist, Late Shri Baleshwar Agrawal was the guiding spirit behind ARSP. He was one of the founders of ARSP and served as its Secretary General from 1983 till he breathed his last in 2013. Presently, Amb. Virendra Gupta is the President of ARSP.

Over the years, ARSP has launched a number of sustained initiatives and organised a series of activities to promote interactions and connectivity with the Diaspora which, among other things, include PIO Parliamentarians Conference, Know Your Roots Programme, Seminars and Symposia on wide-ranging issues of concern to Diaspora. ARSP has constantly interacted with leadership and the people of countries, like Mauritius, South Africa, Trinidad & Tobago, Guyana, Suriname, Fiji, Malaysia, Nepal and Bhutan. It acted as a voice for Diaspora and a vehicle of communication with the Government of India for articulating the Diaspora concerns.

□

Aapravasi Ghat : A Memorial of our Indian Ancestors' Sufferings

— Dharam Yash Deo Dhuny

It is a matter of great honour to welcome and address all of our guests present at this international seminar on indentured labour and the indentured labourers, and their contribution in the making of Mauritian history, society, economy and other related themes. I would also like to seize this occasion to thank and congratulate the ARSP, the MGI, and the Indian High Commission for the initiative they took in proposing this seminar. This seminar also allows us to remember and celebrate the special relationship between Mauritius and India which goes back to the French period or more than three centuries ago.

I would like all of you to remember and pay homage to the sufferings, trials, tribulations, toils, sacrifices, compassion and struggles of our Indian ancestors who reached Mauritian shores many decades ago and their contribution in the making of Mauritian history.

The historical importance of the labour diaspora for the Indian Ocean in particular is that it was the largest movement of population who took place in this part of the globe during the 19th and early 20th century. The Aapravasi Ghat World Heritage is significant because it welcomes the largest number of these indentured immigrants who transformed this small Indian

Aapravasi Ghat : A Memorial of our Indian Ancestors' Sufferings 19

Ocean Island into a garden of sugar and one of the largest exporters of sugar during the mid-19th century.

Mauritius is a nation that comprises of immigrants who came to Mauritian shores from Europe, Asia and Africa. During the course of the seventeenth, eighteenth and nineteenth centuries, three different European colonial powers as well as European colonists have introduced free and unfree labourers. Between the 1630s and early 1700s, the Dutch introduced slaves and free workers from India, Madagascar and South-Eastern Asia.

The Mauritian experience with indenture and the early history of the Aapravasi Ghat, both are unique because they provide important and well-documented insights into the nature and dynamics of post-emancipation societies which emerged in the European colonial plantation world during the 19th century. After all, the indenture labour system created a distinctive pluri-cultural society in Mauritius. Indentured immigration in British Mauritius symbolises the successful interaction and peaceful co-existence of communities of Asian, African and European, which has led to the emergence of a Mauritian pluri-ethnic society.

The Aapravasi Ghat Trust Fund every year commemorates the arrival of indentured labourers on 2nd November and we are thankful to the Mentor Minister and Former Prime Minister Right Hon. Sir A. Jugnauth, who declared this day as a Public Holiday. There are several projects that have been realised and are in the process of being completed in the near future with the support of the Minister of Arts and Culture and our current Prime Minister Pravind Kumar Jugnauth. Some of these projects are the UNESCO International Indentured Labour Route Project, the Local and Economic Development Plan, the inscription of the Indenture Archives of the Republic of Mauritius on UNESCO's memory of the World Register, and the Geet Gawai on UNESCO's masterpieces of intangible cultural heritage. In the context of the celebration of the 50th

Anniversary of Independence of the Republic of Mauritius, the Air Mauritius will be naming one of its aircraft 'Aapravasi Ghat'.

Without a doubt, these projects will further consolidate and enhance the position of AGTF, the Aapravasi Ghat World Heritage Site and Mauritius on the international map of research, cultural heritage and tourism.

Lastly, I take this opportunity to wish you a pleasant and memorable regional seminar in our company.

□

The Tradition of Hardwork, Tolerance and Resilience

—(Rt.) Hon. Sir Anerood Jugnauth

Honourable Ministers
The Indian High Commissioner in Mauritius
The President of Antar-Rashtriya Sahayog Parishad, Bharat,
The Chairperson of the Mahatma Gandhi Institute,
The Chairperson of the Aapravasi Ghat Trust Fund,
Distinguished Guests,
Ladies and Gentlemen!

Bharat aur anek deshon se aaye mere bhaiyon aur behenon! aap sabko mera Namaskaar

First of all, I wish to thank the President and the Secretary General of Antar-Rashtriya Sahayog Parishad (ARSP) for inviting me to attend the inaugural session of this International Conference which, I understand, will focus on the contribution of Indian indentured immigrants in Mauritian Nation-Building.

I recall that in 2009, I inaugurated the Pravasi Bhawan, headquarters of ARSP in New Delhi and still cherish the memories of that function, where we had discussions on the role of the Indian Diaspora world-wide. I seize this opportunity to once again congratulate ARSP for the wonderful work it is undertaking to highlight the role and contribution of People of Indian Origin across the globe.

22 *Diaspora and Nation-Building*

Let me extend a warm welcome to all the delegates, especially the foreign delegates, who, I am sure, will enjoy their stay in Chhota Bharat, as Mauritius is called in India ever since late Prime Minister of India, Shrimati Indira Gandhi referred to Mauritius as 'Little India' during her first visit to this land. Many Indians now also refer to Mauritius as 'Ek Aur Bharat' to emulate Prime Minister Shri Narendra Modi's presentation of Mauritius during his visit here in March 2015.

The depth, strength and uniqueness of the Mauritius-India relationship were described by the former High Commissioner of India in Mauritius, His Excellency Shri Anup Kumar Mugdal, in the following terms:

[I quote] *"Every Indian is enamoured with Mauritius. The extraordinary nature of the India-Mauritius relationship is one that transcends politics, economics or other developments. It is rooted in our common heritage and our common vision for the future"*. [Unquote]

I fully concur with him and with the present High Commissioner of India who has similar appreciation of our special ties. We are thankful to Mother India for the continued support it is providing to Mauritius to pursue its modernisation and socio-economic development. We also express our thanks to His Excellency Shri Abhay Thakur for his constant and enthusiastic efforts to further strengthen and broaden the India-Mauritius relationship.

I wish to tell you that we, in Mauritius, are very proud of our Bharat Mata origin. And at such a gathering, we cannot forget to pay tribute to our ancestors who came as indentured labourers from India and who shaped the destiny of this country with their sweat and blood.

Indo-Trinidadian Poet and Nobel laureate of Literature, V.S. Naipaul rightly said: I quote – *"The indentured labourers are our ancestors, we carry their names, their blood flows through our veins, they form an integral part of our origins and*

The Tradition of Hardwork, Tolerance and Resilience 23

identities, our history is a continuation of their history...as we are their inheritors..." [un quote].

The indenture labour system was introduced in Mauritius in the aftermath of the abolition of slavery. It was termed 'The Great Experiment' by the then British rulers.

The first 36 indentured labourers from Chhota Nagpur in India were brought to Mauritius through the Port of Calcutta on 2nd November 1834. They landed at the 'Aapravasi Ghat' which is a World Heritage Site and a tangible and powerful symbol of the historical bonds that exist between Mauritius and India.

The Ghat is a unique place in time and space where, between 1849 and 1910, more than 400,000 Indian labourers first set foot on Mauritian shores and were processed before being sent to work on the island's sugar estates.

The majority of indentured labourers, 'Girmitiyas' as we called them, hailed from Awadh, Bihar, Bengal and Orissa. Others came from Andhra Pradesh, Tamil Nadu and Maharashtra. They were told that they would find gold under the rocks in Mauritius. Although they did not find gold, they toiled and sweated to make Mauritius a golden island, a country which their descendants transformed into a world-acclaimed model of socio-economic development which is geared by our intellectual capital, knowledge and skills.

Indeed, we are their proud inheritors and the values and qualities they have bestowed upon us, namely hard work, sacrifices, discipline, tolerance and perseverance continue to guide our actions and drive our successes.

The Mauritian experience with indenture and the early history of the Aapravasi Ghat are unique because they provide important and well-documented insights into the nature and dynamics of post-emancipation societies which emerged in the European colonial plantation world during the 19th century.

24 *Diaspora and Nation-Building*

The success of indentured labour immigration in Mauritius led plantation owners in other parts of the British Empire as well as in other parts of the European colonial plantation world to emulate the Mauritian 'Great Experiment'. Between the 1840s and 1870s, Guyana, Trinidad, Fiji, Jamaica, South Africa and many other European colonies began to introduce indentured labourers. Dozens of ships bound for the Caribbean and South Africa stopped at Mauritius.

Between the mid-19th century and early 20th century, more than two million indentured labourers left India, South-East Asia, China, Africa, Java and Melanesia for various parts of the British, French and Dutch colonial empires. More than 1.2 million of these labourers came from India and were sent to work in the Caribbean, southern and eastern Africa, the Indian Ocean, South East Asia, and the South Pacific. In this process, these indentured workers created a global indentured diaspora.

In fact, the indenture labour system, of which Indian indentured labour was a major component, led to the genesis of a new world economic order which exists to this day.

Today, Ladies and Gentlemen, it is internationally recognised that People of the Indian Origin have successfully paved their way to the highest professional, economic, scientific, technological and political spheres across many countries in the World. They represent one of the knowledge powerhouses of the world's developed and developing nations.

Today, Indian knowledge Gurus are actively shaping many countries' present and future with the legendary Indian touch of excellence and sublime dedication.

We, in Mauritius, are blessed to benefit from India and the Indian diaspora expertise in many economic sectors. From labourers in the sugar cane fields, the descendants of the 'Girmitiyas' have become politicians, Prime Ministers, administrators, teachers, lecturers, professionals, financial

The Tradition of Hardwork, Tolerance and Resilience 25

specialists, IT technicians and programmers, amongst other distinguished careers. They are building the new Mauritius alongside descendants of immigrants who came to Mauritius from Africa, Europe and China.

I always say that our unity in diversity and our capacity to respond and adapt to challenges are our main strengths. We have had a history of constant struggle and challenges. But, thanks to the DNA of resilience that our forefathers have transmitted to us, we have always fought against all odds and attained our goals.

One thing I would like to say before concluding is that, Mauritius would have never been what it is today if our history had not been shaped by the contribution of the Indentured labourers and their descendants.

On this note, I wish you a fruitful conference and thank you for your kind attention.

Dhanyavaad

□

The Rise and Growth of Indians as a Political Force in Mauritius and Fiji: A Comparative Overview

—Dr. Amba Pande

The Indenture system led to transportation of labour from India to several plantation colonies. Both Mauritius and Fiji received large number of such labourers from Bihar, UP and several other parts of India. In both the countries the Indian indentured labourers have played extremely significant role in economic, political and social development. Their role in Independence and establishment of democracy in both Mauritius and Fiji have been especially remarkable and deserve special attention. In both the countries, Indians strove for their pride, equality, and their rightful place and has a long history of continuous and sustained struggle through peasant and labour movements which led to the growth of political awareness and community cohesiveness among them. Nevertheless, on the one hand geographical proximity with India and India's continuous interest in the Indian Ocean region helped the Indian community in Mauritius assert their presence and emerge stronger, in the case of Fiji, on the other hand, being far situated from India and India's minimum interest in the far-flung Pacific region, left the Indian community in despair and difficulty. They have faced racial discrimination, coups and as a result have migrated from Fiji in large numbers. My paper seeks to highlight the growth of political awareness among the Indians and their emergence as a political force in Mauritius and Fiji in a comparative framework. The paper will also discuss the peasant and labour movements in both the countries, which ultimately helped Indians in their political strife.

Indians and their Struggle in Mauritius

The island which we call Mauritius today was initially a French colony by the name Isle de France. In 1810, it was captured by the English and was named as Mauritius. By the time the British took over, Indian traders, labourers, houseboys, jewellers, and shoemakers were already present on the island along with labourers from other parts of the British Empire. Between 1834 and 1921, around 4,50,000 labourers were transported to Mauritius which was also the first British colony to import 'free labour' on a large scale. Of the total Indian labourers, nearly thirty percent eventually returned to India, while the remaining continued to stay on. They settled on the lands they had bought and made impressive progress economically. New identities were shaped based on the socio-cultural realities of the time and space. Even when the indentured migration stopped the free passage, Indians continued travelling in large numbers to Mauritius. Indians in Mauritius are a diverse community forming mainly of 'Hindoos' (Hindi- and Bhojpuri-speaking), Tamils, and Telugus (who, too are mainly Hindus) and, of course, Muslims.

The labourers had several grievances related to working and living conditions. A Germen named Adolph von Plevitz helped them write a petition to the Governor Gordon in 1871. As a result, a commission was appointed and, in 1872, two lawyers were sent to look into the complaints of the labourers and introduced several measures to address them. This petition is one of the most important documents in the

28 *Diaspora and Nation-Building*

history of indentured labour in Mauritius and the ultimate statement of their discontent and resistance against the system. Resistance had continued all through the indentured and the period after that. Thousands of indentured and ex-indentured labourers arose against colonial laws, terrible living and working conditions and the arbitrary authority of the island's elite. The workers absented themselves illegally from their work or just deserted or escaped from the sugar estates which were seen by colonial official's offense or crime as vagrancy. The labourers also made effective use of law to show their resistance. Between 1860 and 1886, the laborers filed 110,940 complaints, against their employers in the colony's law courts for non payment of wages, poor working, and living conditions and ill-treatment etc.

Mahatma Gandhi visited Mauritius in 1901 and encouraged the Indians to take up education and participate in politics more actively. Later, he also sent a lawyer, Manilal Doctor to help the Indians against their plight. The decade of 1910 saw large scale political unrest in Mauritius. The discontent was against the sugarcane landowners and also for more political rights and right to vote. The leader of this movement was Dr. Eugène Laurent, mayor of Port Louis, and Action Libérale, During the World War-I, many Mauritians fought along with the allied forces. During the war period, sugar prices boomed, helping the Mauritian economy in a big way. In 1919, the Mauritius Sugar Syndicate came into being, and it included 70% of all sugar producers. Labour party was formed in 1930s by Dr. Maurice Curé. Labour Day was celebrated in which 30,000 workers took part sacrificing their one day's wage. As a result of these struggles, in 1937, Ramgoolam was nominated as the member of the Legislative Council. A cultural angle was added to the political struggle through another movement called 'Jan Andolan' under Pundit Bissoondoyal. Another prominent leader was Pundit Sahadeo who worked among the rural working class. Arya Samaj also

The Rise and Growth of Indians as a Political Force... 29

played an active role and became the rallying point for the Hindus. It helped them in political and cultural consolidation. It believed in mass upliftment and operated through 'Baithaks' (See Hookoomsing 2011). The first general elections were held on 9 August 1948 and were won by the Labour Party. Again, in 1953, Labour Party came to power with better position. Labour Party's continued demand for Universal Suffrage resulted in its grant in 1959 and Labour Party again won under the leadership of Sir Seewoosagur Ramgoolam. Another Constitutional Review commission was established in 1961 in London and further advancement was introduced in the Constitution.

Indians and their Struggle in Fiji

Fiji had another kind of story, as there was an indigenous population on the Island and there was no imported labour before the arrival of Indians. Around 61,000 Indians arrived in Fiji, as Indentured labourers and majority of them stayed back. After the completion of their terms, majority of Indians took land on lease, made it cultivable, and started sugarcane cultivation and some also started working as labourers in the Colonial Sugar Refining Company of Australia (CSR). According to Sanjay Ramesh (2004), "Free from the shackles of indenture, Indians in Fiji became a growing social and economic force and their organisational skills on the plantation were quickly replicated in other sectors." On the other hand, the Ethnic Fijians came under the protective umbrella of the British under the system of 'Paramountcy of Fijian Interest' which apparently pitched the Indians in direct conflict with ethnic Fijian tribal structure.

The beginning of Indian politics in Fiji relates to the attempts to seek and redress from the problems faced by peasants and of labourers. The small religious gatherings and the 'Ram Mandalis' became stages to air day-to-day grievances and political discussions. Peasant and worker movements

30 *Diaspora and Nation-Building*

started as early as the 1920s and were led by leaders like Manilal Maganlal Doctor and Sadhu Basist Muni. Some of these strikes (like the ones in 1921 and 1922) took a violent turn resulting in a confrontation between the police and the strikers. Although the strikes were suppressed and failed to address the grievances of the labourers or the peasants, they did herald the beginning of a political organisation among the Indians and, thereby, helped them emerge as a cohesive force but also increased the racial divide (refer to Pande 2013). In the words of Brij Lal (1992, 83) "...first the defeated Indo-Fijians realised that to protect their economic interest[s], they would have to become politically assertive; secondly, it exacerbated the social tensions as the government had employed Fijian constables against the strikers."

From then on, Indians continued their strife for their pride, for their equality and for their rightful place in their adopted land. By 1937, the first union of farmers – the Fiji Kisan Sangh was established under the leadership of M.T. Khan and Ayodhya Prasad. This Union challenged the arbitrary rules and policies and began to articulate the welfare needs of Indians. It thereby posed a visible threat to the CSR as well as the colonial state which, in turn, felt that, if unchecked, the Indians could become a problem for them in the days to come. These developments further helped the growth of political awareness and community cohesiveness among the Indians. Slowly the issues of concern became broad-based relating directly to political participation, like voting rights through common roll instead of a communal roll and the principle of 'One Man One Vote' etc. for the election to legislative council (refer to Pande 2016).

The Constitution of 1904 presented the first challenge in this regard as Indians were given no representation. Hence, there arose the necessity to fight for political rights and representation in the legislative council. The government, unable to completely disregard the Indian demands, gave

The Rise and Growth of Indians as a Political Force... 31

both the Indian and the ethnic Fijians three seats each based on communal election. Scholars like Ahmed Ali (1980) and Stephanie Lawson (1991) highlight that the award of more political rights to the Indians was closely linked to the abolition of the indentured system and continued need for cheap labour. The working and living conditions were made more attractive to encourage free immigration of labourers. As was expected, the issue of extending franchise rights to Indians was opposed not only by the Europeans, but also by ethnic Fijians. The government, the Europeans as well as the ethnic Fijians saw the principle of a common roll and the principle of 'one man, one vote, one value' as an attempt by the Indians to eventually become politically dominant. Ethnic Fijians strongly believed that concepts like democracy, by putting ethnic Indians on an equal footing, directly contradicted the ethnic Fijian traditional order represented by its systems of chieftaincy (refer to Pande 2016). Moreover, the population of Indians had increased drastically from 28.87 per cent in 1911, to 42 per cent by 1936 with a higher proportion of the new generation of Fiji-born Indians who were more assertive and conscious of their rights. Unfortunately, the Indians themselves were not really united on the issue of a common role because of several divisions like Hindus and Muslims, Sanatanies and Arya Samajis, South Indians and North Indians, etc.

The decade of 1960s saw several new developments in Fiji. Firstly, Fiji saw the formation of political parties, but, unfortunately, on communal lines. As was expected, it was the result of communal electorate and communal politics which the Indians were opposing. Secondly, the debate over independence began and left the two communities further divided: while the Indians under the National Federation Party pushed hard for independence with a Constitution that promised security, progress and political equality, on the other hand, ethnic Fijians were more concerned about their special status and reluctant to accept independence.

32 *Diaspora and Nation-Building*

As independence arrived and the new Constitution was promulgated in 1970, both sides – the Indians and the ethnic Fijians – adopted a conciliatory approach, compromising on several issues. The new Constitution adopted the system of a communal electorate and maintained the special status of the ethnic Fijians, giving them more seats in the lower house, an upper house consisting of tribal chiefs with power to veto any legislation and absolute ownership over land.

Thus, from the very beginning, the general debate over democracy, equality, fair wages, decent working conditions as well as democracy in Fiji became entangled with the politics of race and ethnicity which apparently helped the colonial authorities (refer to Pande 2016). Since 1970, Fijian-dominated parties, supported by the tribal chiefs, remained in power most of the time and whenever when an Indian-dominated party managed to win and form the government, it has been overthrown by a coup by Fijian tribal elite-dominated forces in the name of protecting the Fijians and their rights. Fiji has seen the overthrow of democratically elected governments four times since its independence. Finally, after the coup of 2006 and a prolonged period of dictatorship, a new Constitution was introduced in Fiji in 2013 and Indians were given equal status in several matters, but they still cannot possess land and are unfairly represented in civil and military services.

A Comparative Overview

Amidst the debate over the recruitment, travel, working conditions, the tormenting plantation life and the exploitation of Indentured workers, one thing that remains significant is that despite all the challenges, Indians not only survived but prospered and made their mark in the countries of settlement. There are many similarities in the cases of Mauritius and Fiji as far as Indentured and its aftermath is concerned. For example, in both the countries, the political struggle was closely

The Rise and Growth of Indians as a Political Force... 33

linked with the peasant and labour movements and with the developments in India. Socio-cultural organisations such as Arya Samaj played an important role in political consolidation and religious and cultural revival of the Indians. Nevertheless, Mauritius had some advantages which resulted in its closer alliance with India as compared to Fiji.

Mauritius or 'Mirich Desh', as it was called in popular parlance, was a place very familiar to recruiters and labourers in India as it was a place nearer to India and Indentured recruitments started very early. Great deal of circular migration of labourers was taking place from Mauritius as it was a short and inexpensive voyage. Sources indicate that between 1906 and 1910, more Indian labourers had left Mauritius than had arrived. Fiji, on the other hand, was a place very far off from India and the last colony to receive workers. It saw very few workers returning to India. In the longer run, Indo-Fijians, hardly had any relations with India, though they were closely linked culturally.

Indians in Mauritius comprise sixty-eight percent of the current population. When the British left the Island, they handed it over to the Indians as the rightful successors. The Indo-Mauritians are one of the richest and most politically powerful descendants of Indian indentured labourers globally. Mauritius is an independent republic with majority of elected Presidents and Prime Ministers were descendants of Indian Indentured workers. It is also considered one of the successful models of multi-cultural society. Fiji, on the other hand, is a racially divided society where Indians are still discriminated against and are migrating out of the country in large numbers. Their political ambitions have been suppressed through coups and discriminatory constitution (see Smart 2000)

Proximity with India and India's continued interest in the Indian Ocean region has remained advantageous for Mauritius. India has remained the closest partner of Mauritius since its independence and successive governments have ensured

34 *Diaspora and Nation-Building*

India's significance in the foreign policy. India is the largest trading partner of Mauritius. The country has long been seen by New Delhi as a 'Little India'.

As far as India and Fiji are concerned, Fiji has always remained at the peripheries of Indian foreign policy. South Pacific till recently was of marginal strategic importance for India. Diplomatic relations were established with Fiji immediately after India's independence in 1947, but India's response to various coups has often been lukewarm and has not been able to satisfy the ethnic Indians in Fiji. In the recent past, India's relations with the Pacific and with Fiji have grown significantly. Prime Minister Modi's visit and the launch of Forum for India-Pacific Islands Co-operation (FIPIC) are significant steps forward. However, Fiji elections are due this year and it is to be seen what India can do to ensure free and fair elections.

Notes and References

1. Bates, C.M. Carter & V. Govinden. The abolition of Indian Indentured Migration to Mauritius.
2. Hookoomsingh, Vishesh Y. 2011. India-in Diaspora: A Mauritian Perspective in JAYARAM N, (ed). 2011. Diversities in the Indian Diaspora: Nature, Implications, Responses, New Delhi: Oxford University Press, pp 250.
3. Panda, Ankit. 2015. When India Almost Intervened in Mauritius. The Diplomat. https://thediplomat. com/2015/08/when-india-almost-intervened-in-mauritius/
4. Pande, Amba (2016) Coups, Constitutions and the Struggle for Power: Contours of Racial Politics in Fiji, in Man Mohini Kaul & Anushree Chakraborty (eds.) India's Look East to Act East Policy: Tracking the Opportunities and Challenges in the Indo-Pacific (New Delhi: Pentagon Press).
5. Pande, Amba 2011. India and its Diaspora in Fiji. *Diaspora Studies*, 4 (2): 125-138.

The Rise and Growth of Indians as a Political Force... 35

6. Peerthum, Satendra. 2016. Manilal doctor: The Man of people
7. http://www.mauritiustimes.com/mt/satyendra-peerthum-12/
8. Smart, Christine M.L.A. Indians in Mauritius and Fiji
9. https://www.hsu.edu/academicforum/2000-2001/ 2000.
10. The legacy of Indian migration to European colonies https://www.economist.com/international/2017/09/02/the-legacy-of-indian-migration-to-european-colonies.

□

Strengthening India's Strategic Engagement with Indo-Caribbean Diaspora

—*Jwala Rambarran*

"We don't speak the language.
We were removed from the subcontinent.
We descend from the lowest rungs of the then existing hierarchy of social class.
We delight in soca music while preparing our curries.
What a strange group we are."
(Elizabeth Jaikaran, "*The Indo-Caribbean Experience: Now and Then*, Huffington Post, December 2015)

Introduction

In July 2014, Indian Prime Minister, Shri Narendra Modi travelled to Brazil for the 6th BRICS (Brazil, Russia, India, China and South Africa) Summit, as his first major international engagement soon after he came to power. Subsequently, Modi has made six official trips to North America, five to the United States and one to Canada, for one reason or another he was not able to take opportunities to visit Caribbean nations with large Indian Diaspora communities.

Some 180 years ago, the steamships Whitby and Hesperus carrying 414 Indian immigrants dropped anchor on May 05 in British Guiana (now Guyana) from Calcutta (now Kolkata), thereby inaugurating a new chapter in the history of Guyana, the Caribbean and, indeed the Indian diaspora. This was the beginning of the Indian indentureship system or 'Girmit' which was to continue for over three-quarters of a century and whose essential features were very similar to slavery. Within a decade, Indian immigration was largely responsible for revitalising the sugarcane industry, the mainstay of the Guyanese economy, from the predicted ruin to prosperity.

From 1838 to 1917, the Indian indentureship started in the Caribbean. When it ended, more than half a million Indian immigrants or Girmityas were brought from India, mainly from Uttar Pradesh and Bihar, to thirteen mainland and island nations in the Caribbean. The Indian immigrants were put to work on the sugarcane plantations following the abolition of slavery. This led to a significant Indo-Caribbean presence, especially in the southern Caribbean countries of Guyana, Suriname and Trinidad and Tobago.

After more than a century of toil, struggle and sacrifice in a hostile and discriminatory environment, the Indo-Caribbean diaspora has transformed from Girmityas into a transnational diaspora. They were living in but were not fully accepted as part of the Caribbean nations. The Indian diaspora still now is maintaining strong cultural affinity with India, even being both 'here' and 'there' at the same time.

Most Indians (in India) do not seem to know much about the Indo-Caribbean people. Even sometimes they are mostly surprised that Indians live in the Caribbean. Indians know a few eminent personalities like Shivnarine Chanderpaul and Sunil Narine who have played for the West Indies Cricket Team, but they generally feel that these athletes must be recent migrants or first-generation Indians. The reason of this conception is because the history of indentureship is not taught in Indian schools. The long distance between the two nations is another important factor making India's engagement limited with the Indo-Caribbean Diaspora.

38 *Diaspora and Nation-Building*

Nevertheless, it is in India's strategic interest to cultivate stronger ties with Caribbean nations. Especially, those nations where a large and influential Indian Diaspora can help enhance people-to-people contact and shape perceptions.

China has been deliberately working to deepen its relations with the Caribbean. It has been leveraging its ethnic Chinese diaspora who have arrived in larger numbers in the last two decades. China's relations in the region are part of its longer term geo-political strategy to establish itself as the dominant economic power in the Caribbean 'Belt and Road Initiative', a large-scale infrastructure initiative which seeks to connect China to Asia, Europe and Africa. Demonstrating its commitment to this ambitious strategy, China recently signed the belt and road initiative with Trinidad and Tobago. The latter is the largest economy and Indian diaspora in the Caribbean India may not have China's hegemonic ambitions, nor may New Delhi want to match Beijing's aggression for business, but if India continues to neglect its diaspora in the Caribbean, it will become increasingly difficult for India to maintain a strong regional presence, as China advances its clout.

The Indo-Caribbean Diaspora

The abolition of slavery in the early 1830s in the British colonies of the Caribbean led to a severe shortage of labour in the sugarcane plantations. Having been emancipated, former African slaves were unwilling to provide an inexhaustible, reliable and cheap supply of labour. By the 1830s, the larger part of India had fallen under British rule, which explains the ease, with which the British Raj allowed the transplantation of Indians, drawn mainly from the peasantry to the far-flung colonies of the British Empire. Moving Indians to the Caribbean's was referred to as a new system of slavery by Professor Huge Tinker (1974) in his first comprehensive study. In 1838, Britain sent the first Indian labourers from

Strengthening India's Strategic Engagement with Indo-Caribbean... 39

the Port of Calcutta to British Guiana (now Guyana) based on the success of the indentured system in Mauritius. This system was later extended to Trinidad, Jamaica and then to other smaller Caribbean islands like St. Lucia and St. Vincent, Grenada and St. Kitts. The indentured system was also adopted by the French and Dutch who took Indians to Martinique, Guadeloupe, French Guyana, St. Croix and Suriname. By the time the indentureship ended in 1917, more than 550,000 Indians came to the Caribbean colonies. Most of them chose to settle in the islands. The 'Girmit', as Indian indentureship was commonly known, had generated the second largest mass migration of people to the Caribbean after slavery, forming the start of the Indo-Caribbean Diaspora.

Most of the indentured immigrants to the Caribbean came from North India, mainly Uttar Pradesh and Bihar. They spoke dialects of Bhojpuri, Urdu and Bengali. The majority of the immigrants to the French territories were Tamil and Telugu speakers came from South India. The vast majority of the indentured immigrants were Hindus, with about one-tenth of Muslims.

Many push/pull factors encouraged migrants of all castes to leave India for the Caribbean in search of a better future. Britain's 'scorched earth' policy against those north-eastern regions fighting for freedom was one such main push factor. Some of the factors of migration included: grim living conditions in regions of North India due to devastating famine, collapse of the textile industry, mass unemployment, changes to the land revenue system that benefited the landowning classes and the British colonial ruler, and the increasing encroachment of the East India Company. The enticement of the Arkhatiyas, the recruiting agents, was a main pull factor. These agents lured many Indian peasants to the city with the promise of relief from the misery of their lives; some were kidnapped or otherwise tricked.

Professor Kapil Kumar, India's most senior professor of history at Indira Gandhi National Open University (IGNOU) having specialisation in the indentureship period, argues that there are several myths and distortions existing about the indenture experience. One such myth is that the Indians who left India for the Caribbean were mostly lower-caste landless peasants. He contends this is not true. Instead, many of the indentured immigrants were those who fought the British in the great 1857 'Sepoy Mutiny' and who had to change caste and name to escape death by the British. High castes, Brahmins and Kshatriyas, were most targeted as they formed natural opposition to British rule. But all castes suffered under the British. In support of his case, Professor Kumar further argues that it is not a coincidence that one finds town named Barrackpore, from where the 1857 uprising started, and Faizabad, a main centre of the independence movement in India is in Trinidad.

Indians continued to come to the Caribbean, despite the cramped and depressing conditions aboard the ships, the penal sanctions for breach of contract, and the authoritarian, oppressive structure of the plantation system. The Indian immigrants relied on their cultural resilience for survival and helped in revolutionising the sugar plantation system. When their contracts expired, many Indian indentures found their return contracts revoked by Britain and, thus, forced to re-indenture or receive small parcels of land in lieu of their return passage. This is why, even though the first and second generations of Indians in the Caribbean still yearned for India, they now had formed families in the new countries and lost contacts with their loved ones back home.

The Indian indenture system was banned in 1917 and abolished in 1920. The reasons why the Indian Legislative Council finally ended indenture was because of pressures from Indian nationalists and declining profitability, rather than from humanitarian concerns.

Strengthening India's Strategic Engagement with Indo-Caribbean... 41

Nearly 180 years later, Indians are an integral, yet often distinct, ethnic group in the Caribbean landscape. Just over 1.1 million people living in the Caribbean are estimated to be descendants of indentured labourers. This is roughly 17 percent of the total Caribbean population. Their numerical size relative to headline Indian Diaspora numbers elsewhere suggests the Indian Diaspora in the Caribbean region is very small and might be too politically insignificant in respect of attracting Indian foreign and economic policy interests, but that would be a very naïve view for several reasons.

First, the size of the Indo-Caribbean Diaspora is actually par with that of the Indian Diaspora in Canada. Where Indians in the Caribbean enjoy an ethnic majority, such as Guyana, Suriname, and Trinidad, their post indenture experience has shown qualities of dynamism and depth through land ownership, cultural persistence, political participation, business engagement and access to education (Roopnarine, 2018), making them an economically strong and influential force. In these three countries, the people of Indian heritage retained both their religion and culture for almost two hundred years after leaving India.[1] But, unlike the Indian Diaspora in the United States, the United Kingdom or Canada, they have weak family or economic ties with India (Badri-Maharaj, 2017).

Second, through hard work, thrifty habits and investment, the Indo-Caribbean Diaspora has progressed remarkably well and among the highest earning and educated communities with high per capita in the region. Professor Bridget Brereton, who specialises in Caribbean social history, sums up the post-Independence Indo-Trinidadian narrative[2], which is also partly applicable to Guyana and Suriname, as:

...despite the discrimination and oppression, despite the contempt of other Trinidadians who saw them as heathen coolies, Indo-Trinidadians continued to endure and rise in the socio-economic scale. Through hard work, discipline, frugality

42 *Diaspora and Nation-Building*

(at times, too excess), strong family support, faith in their ancestral religions and a commitment to deferred gratification in the interest of the next generation, Indians achieved success in farming, business, education and professions. And all this on their own, without the benefits of handouts, government patronage or any other favours)

In Berbice, Guyana and in New Nickerie, Suriname, Indians practically own the rice industry, while in Trinidad, they have become an economic force in trade, commerce and business (Roopnarine, 2018). That power is dispersed across several families, industries, professions and even religions. High rates of educational attainment have translated into people of Indian origin in the Caribbean holding prominent positions at the top echelons of state administration. They have produced Presidents, a Chief Justice, Prime Ministers, Presidents of the Senate, Speakers of the House, and Central Bank Governors. The Indo-Caribbean Diaspora has also produced some of the region's best artists, writers, religious leaders, political thinkers, doctors, lawyers, scientists and sportsmen.

Table 1 : Estimated Size of Indo-Caribbean Population			
Country	**Number**	**Percentage of Population**	**Size of Ethnic Group**
Trinidad & Tobago	470,119	35.4%	Single Largest
Guyana	297,493	39.8%	Single Largest
Suriname	148,433	27.4%	Single largest
Jamaica	70,000	2.6%	Third largest
Guadeloupe	55,000	12.1%	Single largest
Martinique	39,116	10.0%	Single largest minority
Grenada	12,000	11.0%	Single largest minority
St. Vincent	5,900	5.4%	Minority

Strengthening India's Strategic Engagement with Indo-Caribbean... 43

St. Lucia	4,196	2.4%	Minority
Barbados	2,200	0.8%	Minority
St. Kitts	1,100	2.6%	Minority
Belize	500	0.2%	Minority
Antigua	300	0.4%	Minority
	1,106,357	16.8%	

Sources: Central Statistical Office, Trinidad & Tobago 2011 Population Census; General Statistics Bureau of Suriname, National Census Report 2012; Bureau of Statistics, Guyana, 2012 Population and Housing Census; Report of the High-Level Committee on the Indian Diaspora (2001).

Finally, Indians have been migrating from the Caribbean to North America and Europe, creating a second wave of diaspora after the first wave of Girmityas. Since the late 1960s and early 1970s, thousands of Indo-Caribbean persons mainly from Guyana, Suriname and Trinidad and Tobago have migrated to the United States, Canada and Europe to escape racism in their homeland and to search for a better life (Teelucksingh 2010). There are no figures on the exact size of what journalist Joseph Berger for the New York Times (2014) called the 'Indian, twice removed' Diaspora, but there is some evidence to suggest they too are educated, skilled and influential.

Suriname, for example, has borne the second largest Indian Diaspora in Europe. In the 1970s and the early 1980s, many Surinamese, mostly Hindustanis, the descendants of 19th century indentured workers from India, fled to the Netherlands, mainly for political reasons. Today, an estimated 160,000 Dutch Hindustanis now live in Holland, particularly in The Hague. Most of those who left Suriname was already among the relatively higher educated and further increased their level of education in the Netherlands. In effect, Suriname has created its very own large, highly educated diaspora pool that represents a potential alternative source of long-term funding (Rambarran, 2017).

44 *Diaspora and Nation-Building*

Many of the first and second-generation Indo-Caribbean migrants still maintain strong economic, family and emotional ties with their home country; an important channel for remittances. In Guyana, for instance, remittance inflows are sizeable, reaching one-tenth of the country's GDP in 2015.

While labelled as the homogeneous 'Indian Diaspora', there are critical differences among diasporic Indian communities. People in the Indo-Caribbean diaspora and other People of Indian Origin (PIOs) in places like Fiji and Mauritius, do not share the same relationship with India as do the much-feted Non-Resident Indians (NRIs) living in the United States, the United Kingdom and Canada. While the journey of the PIOs to the Caribbean was one of forced migration under oppressive conditions, the NRIs, India's professional elite, voluntarily left for the West in the latter half of the twentieth while keeping their freedom and with the expectation of substantial economic gains. Almost without exception, PIOs are the citizens of the nation states to which their ancestors migrated; NRIs are the citizens of India.

Despite these differences, culture is a key factor that binds the identity of the Indian community in each country. This Indian culture within the Indian diaspora has strong links to India and to other Indian diaspora communities around the world. The Girmityas in the Caribbean have been shaped by Indian cultural customs, such as the Hindu and Islamic religions, music, dance, festivals, folklore, and popular Bollywood films. Even though the community have more in common with other ethnic groups in the Caribbean than with the Indians in India because of a shared plantation experience. Not all things from India were kept. Two notable omissions were caste and language. Caste practices were partially shed during the long gruesome voyage across the turbulent 'Kala Paani' (dark seas) and everyone became a 'jahaji bhai', brotherhood of the boat. British and later independent Caribbean governments did their best to suppress the Indian languages and dialects,

Strengthening India's Strategic Engagement with Indo-Caribbean... 45

which is why many Indo-Caribbean people no longer speak Bhojpuri, Awadhi, Braj Bhasha, Urdu and Hindi.

The identity of Indians in the Caribbean is not so easily identifiable. In the Caribbean, all people of Indian origin are known as 'East Indians', as the entire region is commonly referred to as the 'West Indies' and its residents as 'West Indians'. As Vinay Lal, a noted history professor at University of California, Los Angeles (UCLA), writes on his blog 'Lal Salaam', there is no 'Indian', properly speaking, in Trinidad or Guyana. One may speak of Indo-Trinidadians or Indo-Guyanese, but these designations render Indians into parochial figures implicitly disloyal to their country, and make the Africans the true inheritors of the 'West Indian' legacy. In fact, researcher Thomas Erikson (1992 has argued:

"Indians in a poly-ethnic society outside of India cannot be simply viewed as Indians. They are Indians embedded in a particular historical and socio-cultural context, and this fact is an inextricable part of their life – even those aspects of their life which pertain to their very Indianness."

These assertions are supported by the research of Viranjini Munasinghe, an Associate Professor of Anthropology and Asian American Studies at Cornell University. She did an historical and ethnographic study of an Indian community in Trinidad in 2000 and found that differences of caste, sect, region, language, and religion had collapsed into a singular 'Indo-Trinidadian identity'. Professor Munasinghe also found that India plays a large role in the Indo-Trinidadian imagination. She states that even though Indo-Trinidadians insist on their commitment and loyalty to the nation of Trinidad and Tobago, they also express pride in their Indian ancestry. While the wider society tends to view Indo-Trinidadian identification with India as a statement of disloyalty to the nation of Trinidad, the Indo-Trinidadian Diaspora doesn't see these two identities as necessarily in contradiction. They insist they can be Indian and Trinidadian at the same time.

46   *Diaspora and Nation-Building*

Elizabeth Jaikaran, an Indo-Guyanese-American, in her 2015 Huffington Post article 'The Indo-Caribbean Experience: Now and Then', captures well the cultural complexities of being an Indo-Caribbean. She stated that:

"...their unique cultural disposition is why the Indo-Caribbean[s] are able to culturally identify with public figures ranging from Hasan Minhaj to Nicki Minaj. It is why bursts of Caribbean intonation in Rihanna's voice blanket me in the comfort of my home, while the ballads of A.R. Rahman awaken pained demons within me, crying to connect with a history that was ripped from my hands long before I was born."

Jaikaran further writes:

"Sometimes, I refer to myself as simply 'Indian' even though many South Asians would not regard me as such. It is often just easier to provide an answer that people can easily understand rather than undertake the laborious process of explaining the geographic quandary of being brown but not directly from South Asia."

The Indo-Caribbean Diaspora, despite everything, has been trying to maintain its Indian culture and identity, as much as possible.

India's Engagement in the Caribbean

Diplomatic relations between India and the Caribbean offer the first sign of the importance and attention that countries give one another (SELA, 2014). Perhaps the high point of Indian diplomacy in the region remains the then Prime Minister, Indira Gandhi's, seminal multi-nation tour of eight countries in Latin America and the Caribbean in 1968 during which she visited Guyana and Trinidad and Tobago, two countries with large Indo-Caribbean diaspora populations. Half a century later, the state of diplomatic engagement remains weak. There has been only one solitary high-level visit to the Caribbean since the 1968 Gandhi trip. In November 2009, the then Indian Prime Minister Dr. Manmohan Singh

Strengthening India's Strategic Engagement with Indo-Caribbean... 47

came to the region but only to attend the November 2009 Commonwealth Heads of Government Meeting in Trinidad and Tobago. That was the extent of the visit. The fact not a single sitting Prime Minister of India has made a trip similar to Gandhis' demonstrates a type of myopia. This may be interpreted as disdain for the Indo-Caribbean diaspora, given that India's tone and voice for its relations with the Indo-Caribbean diaspora are left to be determined by diplomatic public servants.

Every Caribbean Prime Minister who is a descendant of the Girmityas has visited India in their official capacity. Trinidad and Tobago's first Prime Minister of Indian descent, Basdeo Panday, its first female Prime Minister, also of Indian descent, Kamla Persad-Bissessar, Guyana's former Presidents, Dr. Cheddi Jagan, Dr. Bharrat Jagdeo and Donald Rabindranauth Ramotar have all journeyed to India.

The report of Guyana's Stabroek News on the visit of former President Jagdeo to India captured the emotional essence of a descendant of the Girmityas returning to the motherland:

"President Bharrat Jagdeo went back to his ancestor's village in India's Uttar Pradesh over the weekend and met his grandfather's sister in what was an emotional visit. He also launched a website where members of the Indian diaspora can get help tracing their family roots. According to reports in the Indian press, the people of Thakurain Ka Purwa, a tiny impoverished village about 150 km south of Lucknow, had been waiting since dawn for Jagdeo's arrival. "Coming here is like coming home," Jagdeo told eager villagers who placed garlands around his neck and showered him with rose petals. "Jagdeo's grandfather lived in Thakurain Ka Purwa 90 years ago. The Guyanese president's visit proved a boon for the villagers, as authorities built a road to the village and wired it with electricity within days of his arrival. Jagdeo is in India to discuss bilateral trade and business ties. Jagdeo lit an oil lamp

48   *Diaspora and Nation-Building*

at a small plot of land that was gifted to him by the two dozen families who live in the village. They said it had once belonged to his grandfather, Ram Jiyawan. Jiyawan's sister Ram Dulari, who still lives in the village, said poverty had forced her brother to leave for Guyana in search of work at age 17. "He was right," she said. "His grandson is today the president of a country)."

The visits of Persad-Bissessar, Jagdeo and Ramotar all coincided with these three Heads of State being invited as Chief Guests at the Pravasi Bharatiya Divas (PBD)[3], an important annual event celebrating India's overseas Diaspora. Basdeo Panday was Chief Guest of the PBD in 2005, well after he had demitted office. The record of other Caribbean official visits to India is not much better, with a total of five such visits to India from the entire region over more than a decade.[4]

Further, while Prime Minister Modi has made five trips to the United States and one to Canada since assuming office he did meet with Guyana's President David Granger, Prime Minister Kenny Anthony of St. Lucia, and Prime Minister Ralph Gonsalves of St. Vincent and the Grenadines on the sidelines of the United Nations General Assembly session in New York in October 2015. Reflecting in April 2018, Prime Minister Modi and Prime Minister Keith Rowley of Trinidad and Tobago met on the sidelines of the Commonwealth Heads of Government Meeting in London. These two sideline meetings between Prime Minister Modi and Caribbean Heads of State were tokens of political engagements.

In November 2003, India had signed a cooperation agreement with The Caribbean Community (CARICOM) or the establishment of a joint commission for consultation, cooperation and coordination. The first-ever India-CARICOM Joint Commission meeting was held in June 2015 in Guyana.

Apart from political engagement, trade and investment, there are other avenues for interaction between India and the Caribbean. Incidentally, the degree of economic engagement is not much satisfactory. The Caribbean represents less than

Strengthening India's Strategic Engagement with Indo-Caribbean... 49

half of one percent of total trade with India. The total bilateral merchandise trade between India and the Caribbean was at a meagre US\$305 million in 2010, before doubling to a peak of US\$611 million in 2015, and falling to around US\$445 million by 2017. The trade balance is currently in favour of India to the tune of over US\$220 million. Foreign direct investment (FDI) flows tell an even bleaker story. Indian firms have ventured selectively into the Caribbean, mainly into Trinidad and Tobago, and concentrated in the energy and finance sectors. Key Indian investors into the Caribbean region include Bank of Baroda and New India Assurance. Lakshmi Mittal, the Indian business tycoon, owned both the largest iron and steel plant in the region. Arcelor Mittal had a majority stake in a small bank, Inter-Commercial Bank, but sold the bank in 2015 and exited the steel market in 2017. Berger Paints and Ranbaxy have some limited presence. Unlike Latin America, where Indian firms such as Tata Consultancy Services, Dr. Reddy's Laboratories, United Phosphorus, Shree Renuka Sugars and ONGC Videsh have established a presence. In January 2012, following her official visit to India, the former Prime Minister of Trinidad and Tobago, Kamla Persad-Bissessar had announced at least 10 Indian companies were expected to invest in Trinidad and Tobago (Trinidad Guardian, 2012). The investments would be in ICT wastewater management, ship-building and repair, business process out-sourcing film industry, fashion, plastics and agriculture. The former Prime Minister indicated an inter-ministerial committee would be established "on the way forward with a clear implementation timetable, sector by sector. On the flip side, there has not been any investment from the Caribbean into the Indian market."

The mere location of large Indian diaspora communities in the Caribbean has not been enough to make these countries a focus of Indian foreign or economic policy. Yet it is in India's strategic interest to cultivate stronger ties with Caribbean nations, especially with those where there is a strong Indian diaspora presence. This is because, for some years now, India's rival, China, has been working to deepen its relations with the countries of the Caribbean. It has done so as part of a longer term geo-political strategy to establish itself as the dominant economic power in the Caribbean. China's objective in every nation in the Caribbean is to support development through investment and trade, and then over time to enlarge its economic, political and security role (Jessop, 2018).

With respect to diplomatic engagement, China has generally made a broader and more concerted effort to engage with the Caribbean than India, including a state visit to the region by Chinese President Xi Jinping in 2016. China's Presidential trip was to multiple countries, compared to a single visit to Latin America by Prime Minister Modi when he attended the BRICS summit in Brazil. Prime Minister Keith Rowley of Trinidad and Tobago recently concluded a state visit to China in May 2018.

In the case of bilateral trade, China is a larger trading partner with the Caribbean compared to India. China's bilateral trade with the Caribbean is about five times that of India. While a few commodities, such as pharmaceuticals, organic chemicals and apparel dominate India's trade with the Caribbean, that of China is relatively more dispersed. China, however, has flooded the Caribbean market with cheap manufactured goods while India's approach is more nuanced. The Caribbean almost exclusively exports natural resources (especially in their raw form) to both India and China and imports manufactured goods from them in return.

Unlike India, China is playing a rising role in financing the economies of the Caribbean. China's loan commitments to Caribbean governments for the period 2015-2016 were almost US$6 billion (UNECLAC, 2018), focussed on infrastructure, energy and, to a lesser extent, trade funding. The China Development Bank and the Export-Import Bank of China are national institutions providing almost all of China's

Strengthening India's Strategic Engagement with Indo-Caribbean... 51

development funding in the context of the Belt and Road Initiative.

At the First Ministerial Meeting of the Forum of China and the Community of Latin America and Caribbean States (CELAC), held in 2015, the Chinese Government announced that over the next decade, the country would increase its trade with Latin America and the Caribbean to US$500 billion and would make investments in the region in the amount of US$250 billion (mostly in infrastructure projects). At the Second Ministerial Meeting of the China-CELAC Forum, which took place in January 2018, China indicated that it will not only extend its Belt and Road Initiative to CELAC members, but would advance its relations on a flexible basis in ways that go far beyond trade and development.

Following on this announcement, on May 14th, 2018, China deepened its relationship with Trinidad and Tobago, the largest economy in the Caribbean and the country with the largest Indo-Caribbean Diaspora, after both countries signed a Memorandum of Understanding that makes Trinidad and Tobago the first country from the Caribbean to partner in China's Belt and Road Initiative. Speaking following a meeting in Beijing with Trinidad and Tobago's Prime Minister Keith Rowley, President Xi of China said, "China stands ready to strengthen cooperation with Trinidad and Tobago under the Belt and Road Initiative and help promote its socio-economic development." He also said that Beijing sees Trinidad and Tobago as "a major country in the Caribbean region and is an important partner of China in the region." Official reports quoted the Chinese Premier, Li Keqiang, as saying that China is willing to enhance co-operation in infrastructure construction, energy, finance and agriculture in Trinidad and Tobago and was willing to encourage Chinese companies to invest in the country (Jessop, 2018).

There is hardly any doubt that China's aggressive global agenda, views the Caribbean as an important theatre. On the

52 *Diaspora and Nation-Building*

symbolic front, greater engagement with the Caribbean bloc serves to challenge the hegemony long exercised by the United States in the region. It is in the interest of Caribbean nations to take the China opportunity that promises infrastructure development and connectivity. Like Nehru and Mao in the 1950s, Modi and Xi Jinping today are trying to strengthen Indo-Sino relations, in the spirit of 'Hindi Chini Bhai Bhai' (India and China are brothers). But as Sergey Radchenko warns in his September 2014 Foreign Policy article, great friendships are easier declared than sustained. For India, the overreaching claw of China's Belt and Road Initiative threatens its efforts at building greater partnerships with the Caribbean. India's interests have focussed on Brazil which has become a partner of India in new groupings of the global south, such as BRICS and IBSA (India, Brazil and South Africa). However, this deeper state-to-state and people-to-people engagement with Brazil should be matched by increasing partnerships not trade with Caribbean nations – a fact which India is yet to fully appreciate.

Some Priority Actions for Better Engaging the Indo-Caribbean Diaspora

In the last decade, the Indian government has been taking steps to engage its over 30 million Indian Diaspora, the largest Diaspora in the world, as a strategic asset India's Diaspora engagement policy has been guided by the Laxmi Mall Singhvi Commission's High Level Report on the Indian Diaspora. In September 2000, the Government of India set up a high-level committee under the chairmanship of Dr. Singhvi, an eminent jurist, former member of the Indian parliament, and the longest-serving High Commissioner of India to the United Kingdom, to recommend measures for building a constructive relationship with the global Indian Diaspora. These include launching of a Persons of Indian Origin (PIO) Card which gave visa-free travel and other benefits to cardholders, constituting a High-Level Committee to recommend on how to

Strengthening India's Strategic Engagement with Indo-Caribbean... 53

better connect with the Indian Diaspora, celebrating Pravasi Bharatiya Divas every January 9th to mark the contribution of the Indian Diaspora towards the development of India, and creating a new ministry - the Ministry of Overseas Indian Affairs (MOIA) – dedicated to all Diaspora-related matters.

Since Prime Minister Narendra Modi came to power in 2014, he has been frenetically strengthening New Delhi's economic relations with the Indian Diaspora, merging the MOIA with the Ministry of External Affairs since most of the work of MOIA was done through missions abroad and converting the PIO Card to an Overseas Citizen of India (OCI) scheme which gives non-Indian citizens a lifetime visa to live and work in India with few restrictions.

In 2012, the independent Washington D.C. think tank, The Migration Policy Institute, released a new handbook *Developing a Road Map for Engaging the Diasporas in Development*. The Handbook offers a strategic road map which governments can use to build a constructive relationship with their Diaspora. The Handbook has outlined 'Six Actions to Facilitate Diaspora Engagement'. Table 2 below summarises the status of Indian Diaspora engagement strategy in each of these areas and their relevance to the Indo-Caribbean Diaspora. It shows that while India has a mature and well-developed policy framework for engaging its overseas Indian communities, these initiatives are of little relevance to the Indo-Caribbean Diaspora.

So, while India has proactively reached out to its diasporic communities worldwide, its weak engagement across the Atlantic Ocean and the subsequent lukewarm responses from the Indo-Caribbean Diaspora suggest a more nuanced, tailored strategy is required. One reason for this frail engagement is that India's Diaspora strategy does not take account of the unique 'Indianness' cultural identity of the Indo-Caribbean Diaspora. Another reason is that India's Diaspora strategy does not explicitly target 'biculturals'. Diasporas are composed of individuals called 'biculturals' who have different sets of

54 *Diaspora and Nation-Building*

identities and perceptions towards home and host countries, and who often seem to have an ability to navigate adeptly between different cultural frameworks.

Table 2: Strategic Dashboard of Indian Policy for Diaspora Engagement			
Sl. No.	Diaspora Engagement Action	Status of Indian Policy	Relevance to Indo-Caribbean Diaspora
1.	Flexible Citizenship Laws and Residency and Visa Requirements	India does not permit dual citizenship. However, its OCI Card scheme provides for lifetime visa-free travel and full residency and employment rights for Persons of Indian origin, who are citizens of other countries.	Very Relevant
2.	Political Rights	Voting rights have not been accorded to Persons of Indian origin who are citizens of other countries. However, Non-Resident Indians (NRIs— Indian Passport holders settled overseas) have been recently restored their right to vote by amending rules for registration of voters located overseas.	Not Applicable
3.	Special Property Rights	Indian Diaspora holding PIO or OCI cards have the right to purchase property in India (except farm and plantation).	Not Very Relevant

Strengthening India's Strategic Engagement with Indo-Caribbean... 55

4.	Tax Incentives	Reduced customs duty regime for transfer of residence of Overseas Indians returning back to India are available including the retention of NRI status up to three years after return. Provisions for transfer of funds for philanthropy and tax exemption for the same are available.	Not Applicable
5.	Portable Benefits	Through the provision of SSAs (Social Security Agreements), pensionary benefits of Indian workers and professionals working overseas are both portable and can be totalised in countries where SSAs have been executed.	Not Very Relevant
6.	General Laws	To promote investments from Indian Diaspora, several provisions have been put in place ranging from special incentives for Bank deposits, investments in the Share Market, and certain special provisions for OCIs and NRIs for Foreign Direct Investment. Also, to encourage employment of overseas Indians, amendments to rules for doctors, scientists, academicians and accountants have been or are in the process of being amended.	Very Relevant

56 *Diaspora and Nation-Building*

In the specific case of the Caribbean, India's Diaspora engagement strategy does not cover:

- Indians who have an affinity to the Caribbean (worked/studied/travelled in the Caribbean), but who have returned to India;
- Caribbean students who have studied in India and returned to the Caribbean (alumni);
- Caribbean citizens who have an affinity to India (worked/studied/travelled in India) but who have returned to the Caribbean; and
- Other foreign nationals who have affinity to both India and the Caribbean but are citizens of neither country.

Cheng (2016) argues that engaging 'biculturals' should be the target of any effective Diaspora engagement strategy. Certain studies have also shown that 'biculturals' are most likely to engage in cross-cultural economic engagement behaviour and to assist with facilitating trade and FDI between home and host nations. The private sector is already very aware of the benefit of these 'biculturals'. Accordingly, we suggest the following three priority actions for Indian to better connect with the Indo-Caribbean Diaspora.

First, Prime Minister Modi needs to initiate a program of state visits to the Caribbean region, especially to Guyana, Suriname, and Trinidad and Tobago, to usher in a new era of bilateral diaspora relations, with reciprocal invitations extended. In the Presidential system that dominates governance in the Caribbean, there is no substitute for visits by Heads of Governments. High-level visits provide focus, set policy and raise the profile of bilateral relations.

Second, India needs to articulate an economic strategy for engaging the Caribbean, taking into account the unique cultural identity of the Indo-Caribbean diaspora and leveraging the 'biculturals' who are better placed to use their knowledge and networks to facilitate trade, portfolio investment and

Strengthening India's Strategic Engagement with Indo-Caribbean... 57

FDI. India would do well to extend the preferential trade arrangements it has with MERCOSUR (South American Economic Organisation) and Chile to the Caribbean, create a doing business in India bureau for Caribbean business people, and undertake road shows between both regions. Such actions would help increase trade flows, create greater opportunities for investment, and generate a stronger political rapprochement. The negotiation and establishment of new agreements could boost investment flows between India and the Caribbean. India should use its influence to convince the new BRICS (Brazil, Russia, India, China and South Africa) bank to support financing of infrastructure projects in the region. Conclusion of bilateral Air Services Agreement would enhance direct air links between India and the Caribbean.

Third, New Delhi may consider developing and deploying a core of diplomats who are specialised in the history, economics and geopolitics of the Caribbean region as well as in the unique cultural identity of the Indo-Caribbean diaspora. Strengthening diplomatic capacity and providing sufficient funding to its missions will support New Delhi's outreach to as much of the Caribbean with which it hopes to nurture ties. Opening Indian embassies in every Caribbean country that has an embassy in India would go a long way in deepening bilateral ties and helping Indian companies navigate through the bureaucratic processes that exist in every country, and vice versa.

Conclusion

In the coming decades, India is expected to become one of the main poles for growth of the global economy. By 2050, it might become the second largest economy in the world, after China. So far, the Indo-Caribbean relationship has not been the main focus of Indian foreign or economic policy, dominated more by cultural factors. It is in India's strategic interest to cultivate stronger economic ties with Caribbean nations, such as Guyana, Suriname and Trinidad and Tobago which have

58 *Diaspora and Nation-Building*

large, politically significant Indian diaspora communities. This is because India's rival superpower neighbour, China, has been deliberately working to establish itself as the dominant economic power in the Caribbean through its 'Belt and Road Initiative', leveraging its ethnic Chinese diaspora who have arrived in larger numbers in the last two decades. China's steadily growing presence and influence in the Caribbean should be enough of an incentive to drive the Indian government to take more immediate and proactive measures to bolster the country's ties with the Indo-Caribbean nations.

The challenge for India is how to engage itself in a region that China has similarly set its eyes on. Here India has one major advantage over China and other superpowers when it comes to dealing with the Caribbean. India does not have a history of trying to undermine governments or subvert national economies. This gives India the opportunity to approach its dealings with Caribbean nations from a long-term partnership with the region, rather than only looking at possible short-term economic gains. Prime Minister Modi's tweet on June 1, 2018 aptly sums up India's mantra of engagement: respect, dialogue, cooperation, peace and prosperity. This is synonymous with the Indian age-old concepts of Vasudhaiva Kutumbakam (the world is a family) and Sarva Dharma Sambhav (equal respect for all faiths).

Here too is where the Indo-Caribbean Diaspora can play a meaningful strategic role in nation-building across both regions. The way forward seems clear: it calls for the formulation of an engagement strategy involving more frequent high-level visits to the Caribbean, starting with Prime Minister Modi; a concrete agenda tailored to the unique cultural identity of the Indo-Caribbean Diaspora and leveraging the 'biculturals' who can adeptly navigate between cultural spaces is critical for India to maintain a strong presence in the Caribbean; assignment and coordination of specific responsibilities between the Indian/ Caribbean ministries responsible for external affairs and their

Strengthening India's Strategic Engagement with Indo-Caribbean... 59

missions; and constant follow-up to ensure sight is not lost of the strategic goals.

Notes and References

1. Asia Society, 2002, 'The Indian Community in Trinidad: An Interview with Viranjini Munasinghe', www.asiasociety.org, accessed June 1, 2018.
2. Badri-Maharaj, Sanjay, 2017, 'India's Relations with the Latin America-Caribbean Region: Prospects and Constraints', IDSA Occasional Paper No.45, Institute for Defence Studies and Analyses, New Delhi, India.
3. Bhojwani, Deepak, 2016, 'A Strategy for India in Latin America and the Caribbean', Policy Brief 02/02, Ananta Aspen Centre, New Delhi, India.
4. Chand, Masud, 2009, 'How Does the Indian Diaspora Help Drive Trade and Investment Ties Between India and North America? An Exploratory Study', Simon Fraser University.
5. Cheng, Jonathan, 2016, 'Engaging Diasporas: The Case of Australia and Other Key Countries', Report for Securing Australia's Future project 11 'Australia's Diaspora Advantage: Realising the potential for building transnational business networks with Asia' on behalf of the Australian Council of Learned Academies, Melbourne Australia, www.acola.org.au.
6. Erikson, Thomas, 1992, 'Indians in New Worlds: Mauritius and Trinidad', Social and Economic Studies, Vol.41, No. 1 March 1992.
7. Jessop, David. 2018, 'China's Growing Regional Role', Trinidad Express, May 19, 2018.
8. Kumar, Kapil, 2017, 'Challenging the Myths and Distortions of Indenture History: The Suppressed Realities', Address at Global Conference on Diaspora Studies and Policies: Challenging Perspectives on the Indian Diaspora, The Hague, The Netherlands.
9. International Organisation for Migration (IOM), World Migration Report, 2018.
10. Lal, Vinay, 2018, 'Indentured Labor and the Indian

60 *Diaspora and Nation-Building*

Diaspora in the Caribbean', available at www.sscnet.ucla. edu, accessed June 3, 2018.

11. Latin American and Caribbean Economic System (SELA), 2014, 'Relations of Latin America and the Caribbean with India: A Window of Opportunity',

12. Mahabir, Noor Kumar, 1995, 'The Indian Diaspora in the West Indies/Caribbean: A Cultural History of Triumphs and Tribulations', available at www.academia.edu, accessed June 2, 2018.

13. Mishra, Amit Kumar, 2016, 'Diaspora, Development and the Indian State', The Roundtable, The Commonwealth Journal of International Affairs.

14. Radchenko, Sergey, 2014, 'The Rise and Fall of Hindi Chini Bhai Bhai', Foreign Policy, September 18, 2014.

15. Rambarran, Jwala, 2017, 'Migration, Diaspora Bonds and Suriname's Economic Development: Tapping into the Wealth of the Hindustani Diaspora', Paper presented at Global Conference on Diaspora Studies and Policies: Challenging Perspectives on the Indian Diaspora, The Hague, The Netherlands.

16. Ramcharitar, Raymond, 2011, 'Underground History: The Persistent, Unheroic Past', in Readings in Caribbean History and Culture: Breaking Ground, edited by D.A. Dunkley, Lexington Books, United Kingdom.

17. Roopnarine, Lomarsh, 2018, The Indian Caribbean: Migration and Identity in the Diaspora, University Press of Mississippi, Jackson, Mississippi, United States of America.

18. Singh, Alwyn Didar, 2012, 'Working with the Diaspora for Development: Policy Perspectives from India', CARIM-India Research Report, Robert Schuman Centre for Advanced Studies, European University Institute.

19. Teelucksingh, Jerome, 2010, 'Mastering the Midas Touch: The Indo-Trinidadian Diaspora in North America and England, 1967-2007', Journal of International and Global Studies.

20. Tiwari, Smita, 2014, 'Engaging the Indian Diaspora for Development', in India Migration Report 2014: Diaspora

Strengthening India's Strategic Engagement with Indo-Caribbean... 61

for Development, edited by S. Irudaya Rajan, Routledge, New Delhi, India.

21. Tinker, Hugh, 1974, A New System of Slavery: The Export of Indian Labor Overseas 1830-1920, Oxford University Press, Oxford.

22. Trinidad Guardian, 2012, 'Ten Indian Companies Coming to Invest – PM', www.guardian.co.tt/news, accessed May 21, 2018.

23. United Nations Economic Commission for Latin America and the Caribbean (UNECLAC), 2018, 'Exploring New Forms of Cooperation Between China and Latin America and the Caribbean', Second Ministerial Meeting of the Forum of China and the Community of Latin American and Caribbean States (CELAC).

☐

Social and Political Participation of Indian Diaspora in the UK

—Dr. Sheetal Sharma

The Diaspora communities are quite unique and play a significant role in establishing connections between cultures in the contemporary world. Diaspora, on one hand, is an asset, and, on the other, it can be a potential source of conflict in the host society. Diaspora communities exhibit a unique blend of culture and way of life of their home and host country and because of their different cultural, religious, linguistic and regional affiliation, they can also, at times, be a source of friction with the natives and mainstream culture of the host country. There have been instances of their perfect integration with the host society at one end of the continuum, and their ethnic distinctiveness/differences and un-assimilability becomes a factor for divisions between 'us' and 'them'. Drawing from this framework, this article focusses upon the social and political participation of Indian Diaspora in the UK. The article provides an overview of the history, trajectory, social and political participation of Indian migrants in the UK, and underlines the issues and challenges faced by Indian diaspora using secondary data, statistics, and sources based on primary academic research. This article establishes that Indian diaspora has assimilated itself well with the British society along with retaining its cultural distinctiveness.

Introduction

Indians constitute the largest percentage of South Asians in the UK. People from various countries of South Asia, and cultures are typically treated as monolithic category. Despite vast ethnic, religious, cultural and linguistic differences among people and communities originating from South Asia, the term 'South Asian' in general refers to 'Asians' belonging to number of nations in the South Asian region.

The Indian diaspora among other diaspora communities in general and South Asians in particular is now the largest immigrant ethnic group in the UK. The year 2011 census data indicate that at 1.5 per cent of the total British population, Hinduism is the third most popular religion in the country, while Sikhs constitute some 0.8 per cent.

Indian Diaspora: Historical Overview

The migration of South Asians to the UK is not a new or recent phenomenon. There has been a constant flow of migrants (in varying numbers) from India to Britain, but the history of Indians migrating to the UK can broadly be divided into three phases:

First, the phase from the industrial revolution to India's independence: despite being under British colonial administration for over two centuries, there has been a weak but steady stream of migrants from India to Britain which included mainly lascars (seamen or sailors) employed on British merchant ships, royal servants, ayahs or maid servants, soldiers who fought in the two world wars, politicians, students, maharajas, and kings, princes, and other members of royal families (Visram, 1986).

Second, the post-independence phase up to the end of the twentieth century: after the Second World War, Britain experienced an acute labour shortage and to fill the gap, it invited citizens from various Commonwealth countries to

64 *Diaspora and Nation-Building*

take up employment in the UK and, in so doing, help in the reconstruction of the country.

Third, the phase commencing with the twenty-first century: according to official statistics in 2000, the total population of the UK was estimated at 56.9 mn, of which the Indian community constituted 2.11 per cent.

This rapid increase in the population of South Asians in Europe can be explained as a consequence of mainly two factors. First, the rise in percentage of migration of people from South Asian countries because of increasing international migration in the era of globalisation and the second, the rise in the South Asian population in the UK can also be explained as a "manifestation of a dynamic series of inter-connections between the British Isles and the Indian subcontinent which first began to emerge as the British had set their Imperial presence in South Asia, and are now developing yet further – albeit on rapidly changing terms – in a post-Imperial context".[1]

According to Ballard, in this series of interconnections between South Asia and the UK, 1947 was an important turning point. Ballard explains this in three different ways. First, in 1947, British Raj had come to an end and India gained independence. Henceforth, the destiny was in its own hands. Second, it gained independence as two separate nations and which will eventually become three separate nations, India, Pakistan and Bangladesh, each having different socio, economic, and political trajectories. And third, the post second world war period that marked the beginning of economic reconstruction and boom in the UK (Ballard, 2002). Migrants from these colonies included skilled and semi-skilled workers who worked as electricians, plumbers, fitters, mechanics, construction workers, welders, carpenters, masons, and technicians in the ship-building industry. The prevailing economic, social, and political conditions in these colonies also acted as a push factor (Sharma, 2012).

Social and Political Participation of Indian Diaspora in the UK 65

Yet another stage in the series of interconnections is the post-1990 era of globalisation. The last two decades since 1990s have been significant for both, the UK and the South Asia. The 1990s witnessed an era of globalisation and liberalisation, and concomitant socio, economic changes in India. This was the time of high-skilled migration from India, particularly around turn of the century facilitated by various immigration legislation passed by the UK from 2002 onwards under the Tony Blair regime. Indian emigration has since crept up, reaching 17,000 plus in 2005.

Social Aspects of Indian Diaspora

Indian diaspora is a vibrant community, but it is as diverse and heterogeneous as Indian society back home. Indians in Britain enjoy a dynamic socio-cultural life through associations and a network based on religious, regional, caste, and/or linguistic affiliation. Indian diaspora is a miniature representation of diversity and heterogeneity of Indian society and culture. There is a wide degree of religious diversity among Indians in the UK.

In general, religion plays a significant role in helping to cope with life in a strange and new environment. In the case of the Indian diaspora communities, religion helps in providing a sense of group identity and a feeling of belonging. It acts as a cohesive force and assists with adjustment during the process of transition and adaptation. But, there is also a vast religious diversity among the Indian diaspora community in Britain.

Indians in the UK enjoy a dynamic socio-cultural life through associations and a network based on religious, regional, caste, and/or linguistic affiliation. Far away from their homeland, they constantly engage in seeking ways to recreate and redefine their socio-cultural identities. The religious places, cultural association, celebration of festivities together have also become forums where ethno-cultural memories are retained through interaction and co-mingling

66   *Diaspora and Nation-Building*

with people from same communities, regions or backgrounds. Family and kinship networks, too, operate on the basis of caste affiliations.[2] A large number of marriages among the Indians are still arranged within the caste communities. At the same time, there are some associations[3] that are engaged in eliminating elements of caste-based discrimination among the Indian diaspora in the UK.

The first generation remains nostalgic about their cultural and religious heritage. The second and third generations, however, are characterised by a great deal of cultural hybridisation. One can find different degrees of observance of traditional values, culture, and language among different generations. Modern means of communication have also revolutionised the way people bond with each other. Newcomers do not even feel that they are so far away from their families. In that respect, the first and second generation have really felt the pain and emotional trauma of being away or separated from the family.

However, it is interesting to note that despite being part of the rational economic world of the West, diaspora families often retreat to their safe-zones and tend to co-mingle mostly with people of their linguistic and cultural background. There are clear and visible patterns of ethno-specific networking, which is evident in the spatial distribution of population, residential concentration, employment patterns, and the spheres and sectors of economy where they work. The ethno-cultural affiliations are also visible in social and cultural practices followed by immigrants in everyday life like eating preferences, dressing patterns, daily prayers, visit to religious places, festival celebration, etc. Moreover, the cultural communities and associations of people predominantly belonging to a particular region are platforms for them to maintain and strengthen intra-community ties. These are the places where people even look for partners for arranging marriages and alliances (Sharma, 2013).

In comparison to other South Asian communities, Indians have demonstrated excellence in the field of education. Their educational achievements are better and of a higher quality. South Indians have the highest employment rate among all social groups and diaspora communities. According to the 2010 Census, the rate of employment among male workers/immigrants of Indian origin was 81 per cent. Indian professionals are engaged in a variety of jobs in the field of engineering, computer science, medicine, teaching, aerospace, biochemistry, hospitality, banking and finance. Indians own big to medium-sized enterprises. Some industrial giants and hoteliers are listed as the richest men in the world.

Political Participation

The Indian community has also made valuable contributions in the areas of politics and political participation, being actively involved in developments on these fronts both in India and in Britain. Some of the notable personalities are Raja Ram Mohan Roy, Dadabhai Naoroji, Dwarkanath Tagore, Sasipada Banerjee, and Keshab Chandra Sen. Historically speaking, eminent personalities, such as Dadabhai Naoroji and Gopal Krishna Gokhale ensured Indian participation in the British political process from the early stages of India's freedom struggle.

Not just men, Indian women, too, were active in politics. Bhikaji Cama, journalist and campaigner for Indian freedom took a prominent part at the International Socialist Congress at Stuttgart in 1907, demanding the complete withdrawal of British rule. Princess Sophia Duleep Singh, daughter of Maharaja Duleep Singh, was a prominent suffragette. She was a member of the Women's Social and Political Union. Sophia actively campaigned for voting rights for women both at national and local level in Kingston and Richmond and participated in many public meetings, gatherings, and publicity campaigns, fighting for the cause.

68   *Diaspora and Nation-Building*

Drawing from their experience in the UK, a number of activists actively participated and shaped the Indian Freedom struggle. After India gained independence in 1947, the diaspora community started to proactively participate in political activities in their host country. Over the years, the South Asian diaspora has registered an impressive percentage of voters' turnout during every election. As a consequence of their active participation, Indian diaspora has been able to influence local politics in the UK. They have been successful in drawing the attention of successive governments towards issues pertaining to diaspora, immigration, integration, settlement, their grievances and issues related to discrimination and identity.

Over 50 candidates of Indian origin contested in the British general election held in 2015. The general elections held in the month of June 2017 increased the number of MPs of Indian origin in the British Parliament from 10 to 12. In the previous election both the Labour and Conservative Party had equal number of MPs of Indian origin elected. The Labour in 2017 elections had seven Indian-origin MPs and the Conservatives five. Thus a total of 12 candidates of Indian origin made it to British Parliament.[4]

However, despite their general acceptance and their significant contributions in the social, economic and political spheres, South Asians, in general, at times, become targets of ethnic marginalisation, and victims of racial discrimination. Many migrants, after decades of settlement, suffer from social disadvantages, are excluded from civic and political participation. The first generation of Indian immigrants to Britain struggled for social integration because of two reasons: first, the problem of communicating in English; and second, the memories of British colonial domination were still fresh in the minds of both communities. Also, the first generation of migrants did not command much respect as they worked mainly as manual labourers. Nevertheless, compared to

Social and Political Participation of Indian Diaspora in the UK 69

other ethnic and religious communities, Indians are better integrated into mainstream British culture; there have been fewer instances of friction or cultural clashes involving Indians. Unfortunately, there is growing resentment among people in Europe in general, and Britain in particular, towards people from other cultural communities.

Although people from 'other' cultures experience racial discrimination and marginalisation in a wide variety of ways, but problems and friction come to the fore mostly between the Western lifestyle and values and that of the Muslim community.

In summary, the economic prosperity and liberal framework of Western societies is a pull factor for people belonging to developing countries, who face an environment of social conservatism and economic pressures within their societies. Western societies promise to offer economic opportunities, equality, higher standard of living, access to basic amenities, respect for human rights and dignity. Despite a coy acceptance of the economic worth of the migrants, in the recent years, the presence of the diaspora has been one of the major issues igniting social and political debates in these countries. Indians are the most integrated community among other diaspora communities in the UK. The integration of the Indian community has been so harmonious and smooth that it has influenced and established many specific socio-cultural trends. Indian curry is the most sought-after delicacy; Indian films, music, attire, restaurants, festivals, yoga, wedding ceremonies, and so on are fast becoming a craze in the Western world. Nevertheless, despite all these indicators of harmonious assimilation, the Indian diaspora community has kept its culture intact and alive in as many ways as it has been able to manage. They have presented high credentials in both social and political spheres. Despite some issues of social adjustments and tensions between immigrants and natives in the recent years, the contribution of Indian diaspora and their

70   *Diaspora and Nation-Building*

degree of social integration in the British society has been remarkable and admirable.

Notes and References

1. Ballard, 2002:1
2. N. Puri, 'British Hindus Divided by Caste', BBC News, 21 December 2007, available at http://news.bbc.co.uk_news/7156139.stm (accessed on 11 September 2013).
3. 'Voice of Dalit International', 'Dalit Solidarity Network UK', and the 'Federation of Ambedkarite and Buddhist Organisations (UK)'.
4. 12 Indian-origin candidates win UK elections, PTI, LONDON, JUNE 09, 2017, available at http://www.thehindu.com/news/international/12-indian-origin-candidates-win-uk-elections/article18877209.ece, accessed on 12 June, 27.

□

Critical Challenges the Indian Diaspora Must Confront

—Surujdeo Mangaroo

On May 30th 1845 the Fatel Rozack after a 96 day sea journey delivered 217 Indians to Nelson Island. Between 1845 and 1917, 143,969 Indians between the ages of 20 and 30 years mainly were brought to work under the Indenture system, a system characterised by its ambiguity and oppression. The conditions on these ships were cramped and depressing; there were frequent outbreaks of cholera, typhoid, dysentery and measles with a resulting high mortality rate. It is reported that 95% of the Indians brought to Trinidad 'chose' to remain rather than returning back to India. This discussion reviews the 'progress' and the price paid by those who remained. These Indentured immigrants and their descendants have made great progress in economics, business, politics, education achievements, sports and social and human development.

In the early period (1845-70), the Indians were regarded as 'transients' and, in 1917, 99% of Indians were labourers. However, the ties to Mother India remained strong, many Indians began to set down roots in Trinidad which was facilitated by the ability of ex-indentured labourers to obtain and the growth of the locally born Indian population with no strong ties to Mother India. A large Indian peasantry began to develop growing rice, cocoa, cane, all kinds of food crops, and

72   *Diaspora and Nation-Building*

raising livestock. As they were gradually transformed from immigrant labourers to settlers, the Indians contributed a great deal to their new society by practising their rich diversity of religious and cultural forms. Temples and mosques were built in villages, towns and estate settlements and Hindu and Muslim festivals were introduced. Indian dance, music and song enriched the already complex Trinidad culture. The island's cuisine was enlivened by the addition of roti and all kinds of curried dishes. Indian jewellers and workers in gold and silver practised their traditional crafts. Thus, the mosaic that was Trinidad & Tobago society and culture had new patterns, new colour and new beauty from the people of India, now true sons and daughters of the Caribbean soil.

In 1911, one in 10 (1/10) Indian boys went to school and one in fourteen (1/14) girls attended school which is contrasted to the rest of the population with 50% boys in school and two fifths girls (20%) in school. The illiteracy rate amongst Indians was 96%. By 2017, 66% of merit-based National Scholarships were awarded to Indians and 59% of lawyers and 80% of doctors practising were descended from Indentured Indians. Forty-two percent of Businesses were owned by Indians in 2017. Cricket is by far the most popular sport amongst the Indians and many sportsmen have excelled, for example, Mr. Darren Ganga and Mr. Sunil Narine. In politics, two Indian Prime Ministers: a male (Mr. Basdeo Pandey) and a female (Ms. Kamla Persad Bissessar) and one President (Mr. Noor Hassanali) have occupied the highest political office. There are several radio stations playing Indian music and one Hindi Television station. On festive occasions like Diwali many public spaces are decorated and sponsor celebrations with staff donning Indian apparel including the other ethnic groups. Even the popular soca music has absorbed the traditional Indian rhythms as described by its founder, the late Mr. Ras Shorty I (known as the father of Soca and The Love Man).

But, although a lot has been achieved and tremendous

Critical Challenges the Indian Diaspora Must Confront 73

progress made, there are areas of concern that must be studied and addressed. Diabetes is a leading cause of death and disability amongst Indians in Trinidad and the wider diaspora. Suicide, substance abuse, domestic violence adds to our social burden. Ninety percent of civil matters (usually family and boundary disputes) involve Indians. The disunity and divisiveness amongst Indians have led to what is described as the 'Indian Crabs in a Barrel Syndrome'. When interpreted, it says that like crabs in a barrel – whenever one crab tries to raise or elevate himself, he is 'pulled down' by several of his own type. Several pockets exist especially in the rural communities which historically were engaged in agriculture of Indians living under or close to the poverty line. Whether this is a deliberate act of discrimination can be debated but the facts remain the same.

Yes, Indians in Trinidad have made great material progress, but complacency, disunity and divisiveness must be discouraged.

□

Diaspora and Sustainable Economic Development

—Amb. Manju Seth

Introduction

The concept of diaspora is an evolving one and includes both the 'old' and 'new' diaspora. Diaspora has contributed to the economic development, prosperity and nation-building in their host countries. It has also contributed to economic growth and development in their home countries through remittances, investments and charitable work.

India has been actively engaged with its diaspora and has sought to leverage the strengths of the diaspora for socio-economic development in India. The 2017 Pravasi Bharatiya Divas sought to redefine and focus on involving diaspora in businesses, investing in capacity-building, Swachchh Bharat Mission, Digital India and entrepreneurship, including Start-up India. The Indian government is seeking to actively facilitate these initiatives.

The paper will look at the broad issues of sustainable economic development. The Indian diaspora could play a huge role in creating a new paradigm for sustainable economic development, which would be beneficial to both the host and home countries. India could share its expertise with other developing countries for a sustainable future for all. Some policy suggestions will be made in this context.

Diaspora and Sustainable Economic Development 75

Evolving Concept of Diaspora: Old and New

Diaspora refers to individuals, groups and communities of people dispersed from their original homeland to reside in other lands different from their own. However, they continue to maintain strong socio-economic and sometimes political ties with their countries of origin. Further, diaspora can be defined as populations of migrant origin dispersed from their original homeland to foreign countries, but which are connected with their homeland through various multifarious links involving flows and exchanges of people and resources (Van Hear 1998; Vertovec & Cohen 1999).

Diaspora are comprised of a complex and varied mix of people who have arrived in a particular host country at different times through different means, including legal and/or illegal means, and through different channels. These channels could be labour migration, asylum, family reunion, education, professional pursuits and political and/or humanitarian protection. However, irrespective of the time, means and purpose of arrival, the diaspora has become a major global factor influencing and shaping policy calculations in both host and home countries. It has been observed by many, the Indian diaspora worldwide is in an important and strategic position to facilitate bridge-building between the host country and India. (diaspora-centre.org)

International Organisation on Migration (IOM)'s glossary on migration defines diaspora as 'people or ethnic population that leave their traditional ethnic homelands, being dispersed throughout other parts of the world'. Countries have adopted different ways of referring to their diasporas: "nationals abroad, permanent immigrants, citizens of (X) origin, non-residents or persons of (X) origin, expatriates, and transnational citizens" and these terms are used to cover multiple realities. Refugees, asylum-seekers, displaced and trafficked persons may also be included in the definition of diaspora. Victims of conflict and terrorism, who are unable to return to their home countries

76 *Diaspora and Nation-Building*

for an extended period of time, rehabilitated in host countries may also constitute diaspora.

The concept of diaspora is an evolving one and encompasses both the old and new diaspora. The term 'old' applies to those whose forefathers (and foremothers) migrated to distant lands centuries ago either as forced migrants (slaves or indentured labour) or voluntary migrants (for trade) and by and large, the majority of these descendant diaspora are citizens of their host countries and fairly well integrated in the local, social and political milieu, with tenuous links with the home country. The term 'new' refers to the more recent migrants (both highly skilled professionals and the semi-skilled and unskilled migrants), who may or may not have become citizens of their host countries, while still retaining strong ties with home countries.

Indian Diaspora

India has around 30 million diaspora worldwide including Non-Resident Indians (NRIs) and Persons of Indian Origin (PIOs) present in 146 countries. India's global diaspora comprises both the 'old' (who went in the 18th, 19th and early 20th centuries as indentured labour or for trade, and their descendants) and the 'new' (who went in more recent times as students, professionals, workers, etc). India is now deeply connected with its diasporas worldwide and is justifiably proud of their achievements in host countries and contribution to strengthening bilateral relations with the host country where they have made their homes, whether permanently or temporarily. India's diaspora usually assimilates well in the host societies; excel in education and in the fields of technology and business. The diaspora become wealth and job-creators making valuable contributions to the economic growth of the host country, where the Indian diaspora is found. It is interesting to observe that, in particular, the Gujarati diaspora traders and businesspersons

Diaspora and Sustainable Economic Development 77

have made valuable contributions to the economic growth of the host countries.

Sustainable Development and Modernisation

Sustainable Development is a priority in today's consumption-focussed world and has three elements: Environment, Society and Economy or the three Ps, namely Planet, People and Profit. All the three elements need to be balanced so that one does not destroy the other.

As the world rapidly globalises and interdependence increases, the core issue to be kept in mind for economic development is – sustainability. Countries are modernising, based on the western development model which summarises as consumption-driven growth, while pushing aside the elements of sustainable development. These elements are essential if the world is to survive since the natural resources have been depleting permanently, leading to a crisis. Traditional and environment-friendly practices in the developing countries need to be dovetailed into modern planning.

As part of its emphasis on South-South cooperation, India's approach has been to share its developmental experience, which is more suitable to, and can be more easily adapted to, other developing countries and help them in taking technology leaps in the same way that India had seen technology leaps in the telecom sector. India is now trying to leapfrog into an era of energy self-sufficiency and to rapidly transform lives through harnessing solar energy and adopting electric vehicles, both of which are environment-friendly and sustainable solutions.

Co-opting Diaspora for Sustainable Economic Growth

In general, it is observed that the American-Indian diaspora is looking towards India for investment opportunities. While the diaspora in the Gulf looks towards India for welfare issues and send huge remittances to India for their families. On the other hand, the so-called Girmitya or Indentured diaspora look to India for a cultural connect and have a deep-seated need to be embraced by India. These diaspora would also like to collaborate with Indian entities in Science &Technologies' projects which would bring innovative technology solutions and benefits from India's developmental journey.

India's diaspora is at the forefront of cutting edge technological innovations in the US and the European Union (EU). They are setting up start-ups in emerging and disruptive technologies like the digital economy, renewable energies, artificial intelligence, the Blue economy, blockchain, etc. India needs to tap into their expertise and encourage them to collaborate with frugal innovators within the country to ensure that India has an advantage at this stage of its development with sustainability at its core. This new framework should take on board elements of traditional knowledge and practices which have been handed down over generations and are crucial to a sustainable future. Melding the two latest innovations with traditional knowledge will create an environment-friendly and sustainable world.

The American-Indian diaspora is approximately 3 million strong or around 10% of the global Indian diaspora. The diaspora is a valuable contributor to the economic, political and social development of India. This diaspora is highly educated and very well off economically excelling as high-tech entrepreneurs. The number of start-ups being set up by American-Indians is going up every year with approximately 33% of all start-ups being set up by Indian-Americans. These start-ups could share knowledge and set up joint ventures with Indian innovators. Start-ups are an integral part of the 'Make in India' initiative aiming at creating jobs and growth.

Combining the old (traditional knowhow) with the new (high-tech) would be a win-win scenario. For example, the use of blockchain technology to share information in the agriculture sector between all stakeholders to choose the

Diaspora and Sustainable Economic Development 79

crop for sowing (both according to season and demand); using traditional knowledge/methods of fertilising (no chemicals) based on shared information; updating of land records; setting up a digital infrastructure for agriculture and an e-governance architecture especially in rural areas are crucial areas for diaspora investments and collaboration. Other areas include healthcare where traditional medicines combined with access to telemedicine/latest e-diagnostic tools could transform lives; traditional mechanisms of water storage to be revived along with modern water management systems and in general, following the age-old practices of living in harmony with nature to ensure sustainability in everyday living.

Some other developing countries are also at the forefront of innovations with the diaspora youth, who are involved in setting up start-ups and India could tie up with, or invest in these innovators; replicate or adapt these both in India and outside enabling sustainable modernisation and nation-building.

In general, the Indian-American diaspora is looking for investing in India and they have the finances along with an understanding of India. India would do well to reach out, encourage and facilitate investments by the Indian Diaspora making them central to India's growth story. There are some investments by American MNCs taking place in the IT hubs of Bengaluru, Gurugram and Hyderabad (for example: Uber, Amazon, Google, Facebook, etc.) as well as by Indian start-ups (like Swiggy, Ola, Policybazaar, Flipkart, etc.), and the Government needs to move quickly and tap into this transnational entrepreneurship and encourage technology and knowledge transfer and sharing between them. Also to encourage diaspora to finance such collaborations/joint research/set up incubators/start up in third countries like Mauritius, South Africa and the Caribbean countries (Suriname, Fiji), etc.

80 *Diaspora and Nation-Building*

The recently set-up International Solar Alliance with a one trillion US dollars fund aims to accelerate the pace of the production and the use of solar energy, offers scope for joint research, localisation, absorption of local traditional solutions and co-opting frugal innovative solutions. A recent report spoke of an innovative solar solution in a slum in India where a cone-shaped hole was designed to channelise sunlight and enhance it to light up dingy rooms. This should be wedded to high-tech solutions to replicate and increase efficiencies further. The Solar Fund needs to be used for further Research & Development, financing of solar projects and, of course, to establish standards and protocols for the use and spread of solar energy to enable all countries across the economic spectrum to adopt and reap the environmental and climate benefits. As well as achieve economic prosperity through the availability of a relatively inexpensive and sustainable renewable energy resource.

Diaspora Contribution to Economic Growth

The Indian diaspora has been contributing to India's economic development and growth through remittances. Remittances have gone a long way in reducing household poverty, improving education and health, increasing entrepreneurship opportunities and have been a driver in increasing prosperity and modernising societies.

Investments such as Foreign Direct Investment (FDI) by the diaspora in key areas have been an enabler for small start-ups to scale up and innovate. It has also contributed to scaling up both physical and digital infrastructure in many parts of the country. Some diaspora companies have been active in knowledge transfer to Indian entities and turned the so-called 'brain drain' to a 'brain gain' as was articulated recently by PM Modi. This knowledge transfer is important in the IT, telecom and financial sectors (trade and banking) to enable further economic rejuvenation and reforms.

Diaspora and Sustainable Economic Development 81

Philanthropy is another area that the diaspora has been contributing to regularly setting up of NGOs and charitable institutions in the areas of health, education, water management, rural development and funding self-help groups in rural communities. Influential diasporas have served as lobby groups speaking up for their home countries on issues, such as policy, trade and economic disputes, thus creating a support system in the host government. The Indian diaspora in the US played a key role in the signing of the nuclear deal between the US and India. Also, the Indian diaspora have been buying products from India not only for their personal use, but also importing on a commercial basis a variety of items-such as Indian fabrics, handicrafts, garments, spices, food, jewellery (gold, silver, artificial), etc. Thus, adding to the overall two-way trade with India and their host countries.

The Indian Government has taken various steps to facilitate and involve diaspora in India's growth story including setting-up of the Overseas Indians Facilitation Centre (OIFC) as a one-window facilitator for investments and FDI. The India Development Foundation (IDF) to encourage Philanthropy for social development in India; the Indian Centre For Migration (ICM) for conducting academic studies and research; Global Indian Network Knowledge (Global-INK) for transfer of knowledge, skills, etc. The Prime Minister's Global Advisory Council to suggest policy interventions on diaspora-related issues. The Council instituted the annual (now biannual) Pravasi Bharatiya Diwas (PBD) which is a platform to exchange ideas and to address the challenges faced by the old and new Indian diaspora.

Conclusion/Policy Suggestions

The Indian government takes cognisance of the success and potential of its diaspora communities and has been proactive in reaching out and engaging with the diaspora.

Diaspora and Nation-Building

Some gaps however remain with regard to the descendants of the 'old 'diaspora and these need to be addressed.

The Indian diaspora have contributed to the economic development, well-being and nation-building in their host countries and also played a valuable role in the economic development in India through remittances, investments, philanthropic activities, etc. Indian diaspora has been recognised as the intellectual capital of knowledge and skills by the world. With their emphasis on education, IT expertise, etc. have been contributing their bit to the economic betterment of both home and host countries. India, since the early 2000s, has recognised its diaspora as a strategic asset after keeping them at arm length in the early years of independence. The presumption of high influx of former citizens coming to the newly independent India caused a distance between Indians and their diaspora, especially as the country was reeling under the aftermath of a bloody and brutal partition.

As India emerges economically and begins to take its rightful place in the comity of nations, India needs to build on existing links with diaspora and tap into their longing for being invested in India's growth. Increasingly, India is looking to partner with its diaspora across the world for creating the foundation and framework for a sustainable developmental model to be implemented in India and be replicated in the rest of the developing world. This approach should apply to India's development partnership programme under the rubric of South-South cooperation. Leveraging the Indian business diaspora in different countries to conclude win-win trading arrangements will be the way forward.

Economic linkages create stakeholders and, hence, it is essential to build a comprehensive and a transparent architecture to engage economically with diaspora. The diasporas are looking to India to re-embrace them and partner with them.

Diaspora and Sustainable Economic Development 83

The 2017 PBD sought to put special focus on involving diaspora in business: investing in capacity-building, Swachchh Bharat Mission, Digital India and entrepreneurship, including Start-up India. The emerging challenges of creating adequate infrastructure, the digital economy, leveraging artificial intelligence, the Blue economy, blockchain technology, etc., need to be addressed and integrated with sustainable development planning. India's diaspora should be roped into collaboration with frugal innovators within the country to ensure that India has an advantage at this stage of its development with sustainability at its core. State governments need to be mobilised to reach out and harness the diaspora to invest in and adopt less developed villages in India. This is aligned with the flagship initiatives, such as Swachchh Bharat, capacity-building, digital infrastructure creation, etc.

Involving women in the economic and developmental bandwagon will certainly prove to be a game-changer for nations and in nation-building. Patriarchal mindsets regarding women's contribution to the economy need to be changed and it is important to recognise the economic value of women's work in home, hearth, child-bearing and raising, etc., rendered largely invisible on account of social and political conditioning. The diaspora needs to be encouraged to invest in women-centric enterprises/start-ups and women's self-help groups, especially in rural areas, helping to lift them out of poverty and help in imparting a sense of dignity to these marginalised sections.

Roping in Small and Medium Enterprises (SMEs) and Micro, Small and Medium Enterprises (MSMEs) and building sustainable linkages and partnerships across borders through Diaspora companies should be a vital component of nation-building and development in India. The concept of nation-building is an evolving one and economic prosperity, economic inclusion and economic development are the bedrock of a nation's sense of self and its place in the globalised world. India, through sharing its experience with the other developing countries, including Mauritius, Suriname, Fiji, etc., and learning from theirs, would lead to a win-win outcome for all, leading to a sustainable future. In today's interdependent and globalised world, we will either rise together or sink together!

Notes and References

1. www.mea.gov.in
2. indiandiaspora.nic.in
3. Report of the high-level committee on Indian Diaspora
4. Diaspora Studies Journal of ODI
5. Wikipedia
6. diasporaalliance.org
7. www.orfonline.org (Shreya Challagalla's paper)
8. iasscore.in
9. economictimes.com
10. www.commonwealthroundtable.co.uk (Amit Kumar Mishra's paper)
11. www.thehindubusinessline.com

□

Roles of Mauritian Expatriates in the Promotion of Nation-building through Bhojpuri Patriotic Songs

—Jayganesh Dawosing

Introduction

The Mauritian diaspora is gaining grounds in various parts of the world. The Mauritian artists are promoting the Mauritian music and traditions abroad as well. Mauritians are known to be 'wanderers' and the essence of diaspora can be seen in the Ancient Indian Sanskrit text as well:

"There is no happiness for him who does not travel. Rohita! Thus we have heard. Living in the society of man becomes a sinner. Therefore, wander!

The feet of the wanderer are like the flower, his soul is growing and reaping the fruit; and all his sins are destroyed by his fatigues in wandering. Therefore, wander!

The fortune of him who is sitting sits, it rises when he rises; it sleeps when he sleeps, it moves when he moves. Therefore, wander!" (*The Aitreya Brahmanam, 7:15(700 BC-600 BC)*. Just like Indians, Mauritians too have moved almost to every part of the world-Asia, the Middle East, Australia, Africa, Americas and Europe, and are always yearning to return to their homeland, but are never able to do so. (Bhatia, 1999)

Context and Methodology

Samplings

For my paper, I have chosen three songs from three different Mauritian Bhojpuri artists who, despite living in a different land, are promoting their motherland through their artistic productions. I will be presenting three patriotic songs: one from each as per the following table:

Song Title/Album	Source	Type of song
1. Chawranga jhanda	Mr. Lock Sohodeb from England	Bhojpuri patriotic song
2. Mauritius hamaar (Mahima)	Mr. Pravesh Sahye from Italy	Bhojpuri patriotic song
3. Jahan manwa howela	Mr. Abheydanand Beejan from South Africa	Bhojpuri patriotic song

Theoretical Framework

Critical Discourse Analysis (CDA)

I will be using all the three dimensions of CDA, i.e., discourse as text, discourse as discursive practice and, finally, discourse as social practice where the ideological effects and hegemonic processes in the discourse are seen to operate. (Fairclough, 1993)

Questionnaires/On-line Interviews

In order to gain in-depth knowledge of the Bhojpuri patriotic songs in Mauritius, I also prepared a questionnaire for the Bhojpuri artists, which I mailed them. We also had online chatting via Facebook and Skype. The questions were mostly on their settlement in a foreign land, about their artistic productions in the form of CDs/Albums and their personal opinions about the promotion of Bhojpuri. I will discuss about its analysis in the coming part.

Who is Mr. Sohodeb

Mr. Lock Sohodeb has been living in London since 1975. He went there as an economic migrant with the opportunity to further his education. He has a varied career as a singer, composer, lecturer and freelance journalist. He often visits Mauritius. He has produced more than eight Bhojpuri albums and five books among which we have 'The Impact of Mauritian Bhojpuri Traditions in Britain and Europe', 'Biharee Baabu', 'Heera' and 'A diamond of Jasmine'. The selected song is a patriotic song, which describes the unity present in Mauritius. The root meaning of patriotism is the love for one's ancestry, culture or homeland where as the Oxford English Dictionary defines a patriot as "one who disinterestedly or self-sacrificingly exerts himself to promote the well being of his country."

Analysis of Song No. 1: Chawranga jhanda

The composer expresses his feelings to say that the Mauritian flag is a four-coloured one: red, blue, yellow and green. Besides, there is a famous place in Mauritius called Chamarel where there is the seven-coloured earth. It is a famous tourist attraction in the island. It is believed to be unique in the world. It is also known for the lovely waterfalls and fauna-flora around. Though small in size, Mauritius is a multi-cultural island with different ethnicities.

According to the singer, in this beautiful island, people are treated equally, either they are high or low class, or may he be a Hindu, Muslim, Chinese or Christian.

Revival of Bhojpuri Music in UK

According to Mr. Sohodeb, the opportunity for the revival of the Bhojpuri music in the UK did not materialise until the early nineties. That was the time when the Bhojpuri Boys, now known as Baja Baje, had popularised the traditional Bhojpuri folk music in Mauritius. Its impact was great. It had created an unexpected demand for traditional Bhojpuri records in

Mauritius, UK and part of Europe. The supply was outweighed by demand, hence creating a gap in the Bhojpuri Music market. The sudden surge gave ways to new creative productions resulting into new musical waves. The Bhojpuri folk songs were flavoured with a mixture of traditional Bhojpuri and Sega fusion with Western beats and even with a vague hint of Soca. The music arrangements were unique in its quality because a balance between Asian and European vibes was maintained. This can be observed in Mr. Sohodeb's creation of 'Laila Laila', a Bhojpuri Album published by Tambour Music, a British Company, which helped revitalised the declining industry in Britain. As an artist Mr. Sohodeb claimed that this, in turn, created many opportunities for him to sing Bhojpuri songs to diverse crowds in larger venues staging alongside with some of the best-known Indian Caribbean superstars, like Rikki Jai, Ramraji Prabhoo, Sunnyman, Sunder Popo, Terry Gajraj, Drupati, Bollywood Bhojpuri Superstar Manoj Tiwari, Deepak Trivedi and many more. It was all to do with the popularities of the Mauritian Bhojpuri lyrics which seemed almost parallel to the Caribbean and Asian Bhojpuris.

Who is Mr. Pravesh Sahye

Mr. Pravesh Sahye is another Mauritian who is presently living in Palermo, Italy. He used to stay at Bon Accueil in Mauritius and started singing Bhojpuri in wedding ceremonies in the year 80s.

He is a great lover of Bhojpuri language. He is also a social worker. In the questionnaire, he says that one day he would return back to Mauritius as he adores his motherland very much. He won the special jury award at the Mauritius Broadcasting Corporation for the Music Award 2010. He is often on the Italian Press concerning the religious Hindu festivals. He is constructing a temple there. 'Kaun Chokaria', 'Nacha Beti' and 'Mahima' are among his latest and popular albums.

Analysis of Song No. 2 : Mauritius Hamaar

This is a patriotic song written by Mr. Pravesh where he describes the greatness of his beloved country, Mauritius. With folded hands, he bows to her daily. He lives in Italy and he says that he has left his country, crossing the seven seas. He has brought with him the love of his elders.

Mr. Sahye is ever grateful to his country, the places where he has spent his memorable childhood. He cannot forget them as lovely souvenirs of his youth, which are attached to those places. He has brought with him the national flag of Mauritius and claims that wherever he will go, he will make it float in that particular country.

Mauritius is well-known as the Star and Key of the Indian Ocean. He makes reference to this and praises the beauty of this multicultural land where exist temples, mosques and churches, and where people pray in different languages. He makes special mention of 'Pere Laval' in his song. He organised a fund-raising activity for the replacement of doors at Father Laval at S. Croix in Mauritius, a sacred place for Mauritians who visit there for the welfare and happiness of their families.

The seven-coloured earth Chamarel is mentioned for its natural beauty. The famous legend of the Pieter Both, known also as Muriya Pahar: the mountain head'...where the milkman was cursed by the fairy for not having kept his promise. The boy was turned into stone.

In the last stanza, the author personifies the Motherland who is depressed to learn the death of one of his sons who has cheerfully played in her lap. Today, after his death in a strange land, he has come back to his motherland to be cremated.

The Shiv Shakti Association in Italy

The Shiv Shakti Association was founded in 2007 by a group of five families as a beacon for the future of their children maintaining contact with the culture of the country of origin and triggering an exchange of solidarity with the

90   *Diaspora and Nation-Building*

local people. It is also a group which provides mutual aid to both Mauritians living in Sicily and also to small communities residing in Italy. The association is now known as a volunteer association in Italy and is also written in the register of all the volunteer associations in Sicily, Italy.

The Association organises many activities, such as recreational, cultural exchanges, recitation of songs and prayers. They also organise multiethnic feasts like in 2008— 'A Christmas unlike any' dedicated to the Mauritian children and also integrated the local community. They often organise musical cultural nights where Bhojpuri songs are sung, played and danced with great pride. Mauritian cultural troop and artistes are invited. In 2010, Mrs. Rambha Ramtohul, Mauritian Bhojpuri singer was invited. Mr. Bissessur, Lecturer at the Mahatma Gandhi Institute of Mauritius, was invited in 2012 to host a cultural event.

Who is Mr. Abedhanand Beejan

Mr. Abedhanand is the principal tutor for tabla at the Sangeet Vidhya Institute of South Africa. He lives in Durban for more than 20 years. He is a member of the South African Hindu Maha Sabha which was founded in 1912 to create unity among all Hindus in South Africa and promote Hindu Dharma through observing the best principles of the Hindu religion, philosophy, ethics, values and culture according to the highest tenets of Hindu teachings. Last year, Mr. Abedhanand was really taken up with Diwali celebrations in the following places:

1. South African Hindu Dharma Sabha – Diwali banquet at Kendra Hall with Mauritian King of Gammat – Mr. Vasant Soopaul
2. Hindi Shiksha Sangh
3. Shri Gopal Temple of Verulam
4. The Redlife Hindu Sabha
5. Whetstone Sabha of Phoenis – where Bhojpuri chutney was very much appreciated

Roles of Mauritian Expatriates in the Promotion of... 91

6. Isipingo Hindi Cultural Centre
7. Amar Maharaj Hall – Durban

The underlying mission of the Maha Sabha is to contribute to good relations between Hindus and all other communities or sectors on local, national and international levels towards sound nation-building, based on the fundamental principle of Vasudhaiva Kutumbakam (the world is one family). The values on which the Maha Sabha bases its activities are selfless service, accountability, respect, fairness, continuous improvement and unity.

Analysis of Song No 3: Jahan Manwa Howela

This song is a clarion call: Back to your homeland. The author is a Mauritian who is settled in South Africa and he treats diaspora like a return to homeland. He misses his homeland a lot and expresses the desire of returning back to her. He expresses the strong desire of getting back to that particular place which is meant for the welfare of humanity. The mutual respect which one has for another is unique according to him in Mauritius. He describes it as an ocean of love where he wishes to take everyone for a visit. For him, Mauritius is such a place where the heart leaps with happiness and knows immense bliss. Such a place transforms mankind.

Furthermore, Mr. Abedhanand says that only wise words are spoken like nectar falls everywhere. Words of religion and duty alone are discussed. Tales and legends are narrated. Oh brother, let's go to that place where there are immense joy and happiness.

Finally, in his last stanza, he clearly mentions the name of that place *"jahan manwa howela gulzaar re chalo bhaiya Mauritius ke nagaria"*, that is "Oh brother! Let's go to Mauritius where the heart leaps with joy and happiness".

Hence, we see how Mauritius is portrayed as a peaceful country in South Africa. The mutual understanding among different cultures and religions is indeed praiseworthy.

Recurrent Ideas

Categories of Recurrent Ideas and Practices in the Songs

After the above analysis, where the prevalent ideas are clustered and developed into 'umbrella' categories, the following can be concluded:

1. Expression of emotions
2. Diaspora nationalism
3. Primordialist perspective
4. Civic nationalism

Expression of Emotions

The expressions of joy and happiness are present in almost all the patriotic songs, where the singers and the performers dance in happiness. According to Catherine, in Mauritius, the meeting between Indian worlds and Creole worlds, through the migration of the indentured labour which followed the abolition of slavery in 1834, gave birth to a style of music called 'chutney'. As a result of the African influence on an Indian folk genre, chutney music embodies the transformation of music for listening into music for dancing.

Diaspora Nationalism

Rogers Brubaker (2005) argues that, more recently, *diaspora* has been applied to emigrant groups that continue their involvement in their homeland from overseas, such as the category of long-distance nationalists identified by Benedict Anderson. Brubaker notes that (as examples): Albanians, Basques, Hindu Indians, Irish, Japanese, Kashmiri, Koreans, Kurds, Palestinians, and Tamils have been conceptualised as diasporas in this sense. Furthermore, "labour migrants who maintain (to some degree) emotional and social ties with a homeland" have also been described as Diasporas. We witness in these songs a strong sense of diaspora nationalism where despite being far away from their motherland, all the three singers leave no stones unturned in the promotion of Mauritius.

The Primordialist Perspective

In the selected Bhojpuri songs, the primordialist perspective is mostly seen. The primordialist perspective is based upon evolutionary theory. The evolutionary theory of nationalism perceives it to be the result of the evolution of human beings into identifying with groups, such as ethnic groups, or other groups that form the foundation of a nation. Roger Masters in *The Nature of Politics (1989)* describes the primordial explanation of the origin of ethnic and national groups as recognising group attachments that are thought to be unique, emotional, intense and durable because they are based upon kinship and promoted along lines of common ancestry.

The primordialist evolutionary view of nationalism has its origins in the evolutionary theories of Charles Darwin that were later substantially elaborated by John Tooby and Leda Cosmides. Central to evolutionary theory is that all biological organisms undergo changes in their anatomical features and their characteristic behaviour patterns. Darwin's theory of natural selection as a mechanism of evolutionary change of organisms is utilised to describe the development of human societies and particularly the development of mental and physical traits of members of such societies.

Civic Nationalism

All the three Mauritian artists believe in civic nationalism because they see the nation as an association of people who identify themselves as belonging to the nation, who have equal and shared political rights, and allegiance to similar political procedures. According to the principles of civic nationalism, the nation is not based on common ethnic ancestry, but is a political entity whose core identity is not ethnicity. This civic concept of nationalism is exemplified by Ernest Renan in his lecture in 1882—'What is a Nation?', where he defined the nation as a 'daily referendum' (frequently translated 'daily plebiscite') dependent on the will of its people to continue living together.

Conclusion

Mauritian Diaspora is getting itself connected to various parts of the world. Mauritian artists are successful in popularising their cultures and traditions abroad as well. Despite anti-immigrant sensibilities, the multi-faith values are gaining grounds. Religious festivals, religious ceremonies and processions on the street of London, Palermo and Durban are evidence of the tolerance, integration and acceptance of the Mauritian Hindu ancestral legacy into the foreign society. The popularity of Mauritian Bhojpuri language and music are food for thought for the continuity of ancestral legacy. They identify themselves to that particular place where they have voluntarily flown to further promote the Mauritian culture and traditions.

Acknowledgements

I would like to express my appreciation to Dr. Suchita Ramdin, Dr. Sarita Boodhoo, the folksingers: Mrs. Manaram, Mrs. Mathoor, Mrs. Hunsraz and also Mr. Baboolall, Mr. Mohith who collaborated in the research conducted on Bhojpuri folk songs.

Notes and References

1. Fairclough, Norman. 'Discourse and text: Linguistic and intertextual analysis within discourse analysis.' *Discourse & Society* 3.2 (1992): 193-217.
2. Manuel, Peter. 'Music, identity, and images of India in the Indo-Caribbean diaspora.' *Asian Music* (1997): 17-35.
3. Manuel P. Popular music as popular expression in North India and the Bhojpuri region, from cassette culture to VCD culture. *South Asian Popular Culture* [serial online]. October 2012;10(3):223-236. Available from: Academic Search Complete, Ipswich, MA. Accessed October 11, 2014.

Roles of Mauritian Expatriates in the Promotion of... 95

4. Tripathy R. BHOJPURI CINEMA: *South Asian Popular Culture* [serial online]. October 2007;5(2):145-165. Available from: Academic Search Complete, Ipswich, MA. Accessed October 11, 2014.

5. Murphey, Tim. 'The discourse of pop songs.' *Tesol Quarterly* 26.4 (1992): 770-774.

6. Jassal, SmitaTewari. 'Bhojpuri songs, women's work and social control in northern India.' *Journal of peasant studies* 30.2 (2003): 159-206.

7. Manuel, Peter. 'Music, identity, and images of India in the Indo-Caribbean diaspora.' *Asian Music* (1997): 17-35.

8. Bhalla, P, 2006. Hindu Rites, Rituals, Customs & Traditions. New Delhi: Pustak Mahal.

9. Creswell, J.W., 2003. Research Design-Qualitative, Quantitative and mixed methods approaches, 2nd ed. Sage Publication.

10. Ramdin, S., 1989. Sanskaar Manjari: Moka: Mahatma Gandhi Institute.

11. Mohith, D.,2003. Bhojpuri ke heera-moti, Part 4, Delhi: Natraj Prakashan.

12. Myers, Helen, ed. *Ethnomusicology. An Introduction.* WW Norton, 1992.

□

The Role of the Indian Diasporic Intangible Heritage in Identity Creation and Nation-Building in Mauritius

—Kiran C. Jankee

Introduction

Mauritius can be considered as the foremost representation of a successful diasporic movement from India that has established itself in a new land and within a period of less than 200 years. In some instances, Mauritians have adapted socio-cultural practices from India that are still present in their society.

The indenture phenomenon is unique to Mauritius as it ended up being practised in other places, such as Fiji and the Caribbean islands like Trinidad and Tobago, Suriname and Guyana. Mauritius stands out as the origin of the Great British Experiment. Having been brought here as indentured labourers, Indian immigrants here established themselves very quickly within the new space adapted to various social and cultural practices, among them, the extremely rich intangible cultural heritage. These vary from religious to other cultural practices embracing practices, beliefs, rituals and other cultural phenomena unique to the people of Indian origin.

The Role of the Indian Diasporic Intangible Heritage... 97

In this paper, I discuss this rich and unique Intangible Cultural Heritage of Mauritians of Indian origin including Geet-Gawai along with others, which has been listed in the UNESCO Representative List of the Intangible Cultural Heritage of Humanity. Rituals, religious practices have cemented, created and unified people giving them both spirit and sense of place to be able to contribute to the development of a new country of Mauritius which is proud, innovative and self-assured.

For people to be able to develop, they need to have self-pride, identity and a sense of place and continuation. The intangible heritage of the Indian diaspora population of Mauritius has bestowed them with this and today they form 60 % of the population of this island. Their impact through this sense of identity provides them with self-confidence to continuously create and innovate making Mauritius one of the fastest-developing countries in this part of the Indian Ocean and around the world.

Intangible Heritage in the Creation of Identity and Nation building

The Indian culture is a legacy of the Indian Indentured labourers brought to Mauritius after the abolition of slavery in 1834. Approximately, 80% of the Indentured labourers came from India while the rest came from Madagascar, East Africa and China.

One of the most important intangible heritages that are responsible for the development, spread and establishment of other intangible heritage is language. In the case of Mauritius, the majority of the people brought from India were from the Bhojpuri belt, making the Bhojpuri language become the lingua franca of Mauritius. The impact of the Bhojpuri language was immense. As the people who worked on the sugar camps were basically of Bhojpuri-speaking Indian origin, the Chinese shopkeepers, and the white masters would use Bhojpuri as means of communication. Not only was the Indian language

98 *Diaspora and Nation-Building*

picked up by the general population and sugar estate owners, even the last rites and rituals practiced made their way in the popular culture of Mauritius.

Rituals like *Harparawri* for the invocation of rain during drought season, prayers and rituals like *Baharya puja* for good yield just before harvest seasons were recognised, valued and commissioned by the Franco Mauritian estate owners to achieve the same effects. The pre-harvest rituals have now become an official function to declare the harvest season open. The Prime Minister and the estate owners are the chief guests at the Amma Tokay Kovil every year, bringing Mauritians together in the spirit of collective economic, spiritual and social well-being of the country. In every sugar estate, the Indian workers had set up small kalimaye and shrines. Still today, there are many kovils and kalimaye found on sugar estates. While a few sugar estate owners have donated the area of the shrines, others have not objected to people maintaining the kalimaye and the performance of prayers.

Mauritius has gone through the journey of *'from girmitya to government'*. The sons and daughters of those who were brought here as indentured immigrants through sheer hard work have ended up being the rulers of their new found country. A sense of belonging in shared heritage including common religious and other cultural practices helped build Mauritius of today. The immigration depot of the Indentured labourers known as Aapravasi Ghat is today a World Heritage Site. It is designated for its Outstanding Universal Value (OUV) representing a major event in human history that defined a difficult migration process with a successful ending. Aapravasi Ghat today forms parts of the common Heritage of Humanity with an OUV that clearly states that: "The Aapravasi Ghat Immigration Depot is the site from where the modern indentured labour Diaspora emerged ...with architectural ensemble that stands for this 'Great Experiment', an attempt... to demonstrate the superiority of 'free' over slave labour".

The Role of the Indian Diasporic Intangible Heritage... 99

With its main objective to carry out research on indentured labour and sites, the Aapravasi Ghat Trust Fund contributes to research that enriches the history of Mauritius. It also helps the people of Indian origin by providing them self-pride and identity creation. It demonstrates and recognises that the memories, traditions, cultures and practices of indentured immigrants are valuable for the unity and development of the country. In this regard, the institution works collectively and closely with communities to document, protect, promote and disseminate the Intangible Cultural Heritage (ICH) of Indentured immigrants. This heritage is the basis and foundation in which the pride and self-confidence of Mauritians of Indian origin is rooted. It is this self-confidence and pride that empowers these descendants of the indentured labourers to positively contribute to a country they now call theirs, Mauritius.

Mauritius is a representation of true multiplicity of cultures, a rainbow nation that has given visibility to the Indian cultural riches. The cultures of Indian origins have, in turn, given and borrowed from others, creating a plethora of rich Mauritian heritage ranging from cuisine, music, dance, religious rituals and others.

The cohabitation of people of different ethnic groups has created a deep understanding and appreciation of other people's culture, leading to a tolerance and nation-building in Mauritius. Every culture has been more or less influenced by other cultures further forging elements that can be considered national cultural identities. Thus, possibly all Mauritians today eat Dalpuri, speak Creole and participate in Cavedi among all other cultural influences. The multiculturalism in Mauritius has created thriving communities of Creoles, Chinese, Muslims, Tamils, Telugus, Marathis and Hindus. They all enjoy eating dalpuri, biryani, fried noodles, Haleem, rotis, rougaillepoisson sale (salted fish stew) and grills.

This is not to say that Mauritius has no diversity. As is often said, cultural diversity is as good for people just as

100   *Diaspora and Nation-Building*

biodiversity is for nature. Thus, the people of Mauritius are proud of their various ethnic backgrounds and do indeed dress up accordingly. However, in the same spirit, there are many shared heritages that bring uniformity particularly on special occasions. For example, it can be said that the tradition of attending weddings of people of the other cultures started from sugar camps and continues till today. In these cases, people enjoy wearing Indian apparel and attending Hindu and Muslim weddings, as well as enjoying the typical traditional dishes. On the same note, the people also enjoy the celebrations of Christmas and of Chinese New Year.

While some of the safeguard practices of heritage, especially Indian culture, have happened naturally and randomly, in many circumstances, they have been structured. One of the means of promoting Indian culture in Mauritius was through the cinema. The impact of Indian cinema had a great contribution in the safeguard, promotion and transmission of Hindustani language and Indian culture in Mauritius. During the 1950s and 1960s, Mauritius had the greatest number of cinema halls across the country. For example, a village town like Goodlands in the north of the country had four cinema halls (namely Kings, Astoria, Spitfire and New Spitfire) and all of them were fully packed for each and every release of Indian movies.[1] The Indian cinema for people at that time was not just leisure but it was addressing the general issues related to social, economic and political fields.

In terms of dress, it could be observed that between the1950s and 1970s people were dressing up at their best, highly influenced by Bollywood movies and believed that dress makes a man or woman. Through cinema, people learned more about the Indian culture and started imitating and living it. *Heena*, *mangalsutra*, and celebration of *karwachawth* festivalare the results of impact of the Indian cinema. It can, therefore, be said that the Indian cinema shaped the lives of people as they were inspired to learn the language, dress code

The Role of the Indian Diasporic Intangible Heritage... 101

and the Indian music among others. Many people even aspired and became teachers of Asian languages and Indian music at the Mahatma Gandhi Institute (MGI).

While immigration, globalisation and abundance of other public cultures can be positive and contribute to a country of innovation, the same can be a threat to the existing cultures especially when the youth aspire for what is not theirs and undermine the traditional cultures of their parents and grandparents. The Indian cultures are no exception and the Bhojpuri language nearly became a victim if it was not for the efforts of some community members and the government to safeguard it. Thus, the danger of standardisation is real pertinent in Mauritius. To deal with this, the Mauritian government has set up cultural centres and speaking unions for all different languages and ethnic groups. This is to make sure that at least the respective bodies work to safeguard the collective national heritage and the nature and identity of the rainbow nation. This could bring in negative competitions and unnecessary conflicts, if not properly managed. So far, the Mauritian case has worked well in safeguarding unity in diversity.

Lastly, the 2003 UNESCO Convention on Intangible Cultural Heritage of Humanity offers an opportunity for safeguarding our heritage including those of Indian diaspora. It is in this regard that Geet Gawai, the Bhojpuri wedding ritual, has been listed as a heritage of Humanity. This does not only bring pride to the Mauritians of Indian descendent, but to the whole of Mauritius as well as the world community. Under the leadership of the Bhojpuri-speaking Union, and the Geet Gawai School of Petit Raffray, Geet Gawai as an intangible heritage has become a household practice in Mauritius. Today, nearly every wedding among the Hindi-speaking Mauritians, every National Day, every national important occasion has a Geet Gawai troupe.

Most of the District Councils in the country organise Geet Gawai competitions. Since its inscription in the list of ICH of

Humanity, nearly 30 Geet Gawai Schools have sprung up in different parts of the country, playing major roles in the lives of various communities. Beyond singing and dancing, they are focussing the issues on leadership provision, economic empowerment, social gathering and community support to provisions of solace and talent development.

All these examples discussed in the paper demonstrate the power of intangible cultural heritage in nation-building. Mauritius is a good example of a nation of rich heritage including intangible that should be considered as a national resource. In this age of fast developments and fierce competition between cultures, Mauritius should pride itself as one place, where the co-existence of heritage of various origins is real and celebrated. India and its culture have been a contributor to this. Today, this entire heritage including the heritage of Indian diaspora is a sure way of Mauritius gaining sustainable development including meeting its obligations and responsibilities concerning the UN Sustainable Development Goals.

Notes and References

1. Jankee, K. 2001. Recollections on impact of Indian cinema in Mauritius during the 50s and 60s: Goodlands—a case study. Reduit. University of Mauritius.

The Role of the Arts/Performing Arts in the Socio-cultural Practice of Indian Indentured Immigrants: Towards Nation Building in Mauritius

—Dr. Sheilana Devi Ramdoo

The arrival of Indian Indentured immigrants to Mauritius in 1834 opened a continuing chapter in the history of sufferings of the Indian culture. Although the indentured labourers, being prominently Indian village folks, were oppressed, they had been clinging to a religious consciousness. This was the key because this religious consciousness, which was vehicled through socio-cultural practices like rituals and festive ceremonies, was also unconsciously and unknowingly being carried through accompanying traces of Indian performing arts.

No exact, detailed records exist about the modes of artistic expression of Indian indentured immigrants in Mauritius, but they formed an integral part of socio-cultural practices. Apart from the physical aspect, the songs, music and dance often expressed sentiments or moods associated to their daily acts – first, in the profane context; for example, on their agricultural fieldwork, for specific events like weddings, births, etc., and second, in the sacred context, as in their ritualistic prayers and specific cultural festivities, but which also essentially helped

104   *Diaspora and Nation-Building*

to drown their miseries. Did they ever have time or to what extent were they allowed and willing to paint, sing, dance or play their miseries? Some remaining evidences of Indian performing arts through socio cultural practices are Bhojpuri music, song and dance of the Hindi-speaking community, Kavadi songs, music and dance of the Tamil-speaking community; Ganesh Chaturthi songs, music and dance of the Marathi-speaking community and Rambhajan songs, music and dance of the Telegu-speaking community.

Because of the almost fragmentary nature of Indian performing arts which were merged the socio-cultural practices of Indian immigrants in Mauritius, there are four features of the arts/performing arts which will mainly be considered for the purpose of this presentation:

I.   The arts/performing arts will not be considered as an art form, but rather as a process, i.e., an art process based on achieving social outcomes where specific critical social and cultural issues required attention. The arts/performing arts will not be considered as a written tradition that involves transposition of a written text into a performative event, but rather as the improvised and ritualised spectrum of human performance ranging from folk narratives, songs recitations, elementary gestures, spontaneous movements, music, etc., for the purpose of entertainment, everyday life enactment of social roles, gender roles, class roles plus for the purpose of socio-religious practices.

II.   The arts/performing arts will not be viewed here as end-products but as part of transformational approaches/vehicles through which people can engage in the joint identification and production of images, symbols and other resources

The Role of the Arts/Performing Arts in the...   105

reflective of community visions and aspirations (Sonn et al.., 2002).

III. The arts/performing arts will be emphasized here amidst a number of semiotic resources to produce meaning and communicate ideas, values and beliefs; and to construct the meaning out of the dynamically unfolding interplay of semiotic patterns in performance.

IV. The arts/performing arts will be seen as potential resources that provide a way to index a community's experience and to participate in the making of "their own history, their own future and their own identity" (Thomas & Rappaport, p. 326).

These are a few aspects of research results indicating the possible contributions which the arts/performing arts could have made through some form of functional roles, even though elementary and merged together with socio-cultural practices – they were probably not so evident in those days, but today they are growing more and more evident.

They Allow People to Retain Contact with Their Roots

Any art form or mode of art expression naturally draws on tales of one's culture, myths, legends, songs, etc. (Business Week, 1996). In the case of Indian Indentured immigrants, the main sources of these were the Hindu sacred scriptures (They offer a window into a person's soul where his values, attitudes, beliefs and visions are explored and reflected upon. This can be done also through the supportive medium of songs, music, movement, folk narratives, recitations, etc. The arts/performing arts can contribute or could have definitely contributed to relate to the essence of who we are, where we have come from, and where we are journeying. It can help affirm a person's sense of being, allowing people to retain contact with their roots.

106 *Diaspora and Nation-Building*

Markers of Identity

Activities or socio-cultural practices involving music/song/movement improve physical and psychological well-being because they are generally sources of enjoyment – both emotionally and psychologically (Baklien, 2000; Ball and Keating, 2002; Bygren, Konlaaan and Johannson, 1996; Turner and Senior, 2000). But moreover, those 'practices' culminated as the Indian immigrants' markers of identity.

Indentured immigrants in Mauritius had suffered from social isolation, from the loss of their loved ones, a deteriorating health and unexpected tedious life transitions. There is a type of art process called community art process which usually involves people who are disadvantaged, people in a poor neighbourhood. These modes of art expressions become a medium through which communities talk about and express their emotions and their needs. Therefore, the arts/performing arts can be or could have been partly for Indian immigrants in Mauritius, an agent of communal meanings; hence, markers of identity, as they help reinforce a sense of identity.

Nation-building

The process of conscientisation is a key value to community psychology. The arts/performing arts have been found through research to facilitate the process of conscientisation, i.e., becoming aware of limiting social, political and historical realities and, more importantly, acting in solidarity to transform those realities (Freire, 1972; Martin-Baro, 1994; Montero, 2009). This conscientisation process spurs for collective action and collective efficacy. Hence, the arts/performing arts can act or could have, in those days, contributed partly as catalysts for attainment of community goals- because the arts/performing arts have also been found to be able to contribute towards creating community-driven vision for the future.

Conclusion

In those Indian immigrant days, in Mauritius, although there were mild forms or traces of artistic expressions merged into socio-cultural practices, yet today they have served as fundamental departure points towards gradual establishment of the Indian performing arts in the Mauritian educational system and we are still striving to expand them so as to bring them closer to authenticity in their cultural dimensions. Traditional religions have long recognised the fundamental nature of the arts/performing arts contribution to the collective processes of thought, memory and perception in society. This contribution is evident in the arts/performing arts contained in Buddhism, Christianity, Islam, Hinduism – which conveys highly formal integrated worldviews (Merlin 2006, p. 6).

As descendants of the Indian Indentured immigrant in Mauritius, we are today proceeding forward with one and the same identical mindset. But what is interesting about this inherited mindset from our Indian immigrant ancestors is that it is totally in keeping with what characterises an artistic mindset. In any work of art, be it a song, a poem, poetry, painting, pottery, sculpture, music, dance, drama, etc., the idea of standard and quality is the key value. It is essential for an art student to prepare himself to make his present art work better than the previous one, as the art student progresses, a spirit of continuous improvement enters in his mind and, gradually, he develops focussed and sustained attention towards improving the standard and quality of his artwork. This is why, True/ Real artists never stop in their progression. Whatever level they reach, artists are engaged continuously into improving their work, there is non-stop engagement towards raising the standard and quality of one's art work.

The reason for this is very simple because an artistic mind always targets for perfection. Perfection is huge and infinite, and because it is infinite, many call It God. Even if we know, we

108　　　　　　　*Diaspora and Nation-Building*

can't or it is too difficult to reach this Perfection, we still strive to near it. And this is partly the reason for which we believe firmly in the value of making efforts to achieve.

I personally believe this is the most precious treasure we have all inherited from our indentured immigrant ancestors from India.

Notes and References

1. Business Week, 1996. *'The Changing Workplace is Changing Our View of Education'.*
2. Creative City Network of Canada with the Support of Canada Council for the Arts,. *'ARTS and positive change in communities'* [www.creativecity.ca/resources/making-the-case/]
3. Dolan, T., 1995. *'Community Arts: Helping to Build Communities? Taken from a Southern Ireland perspective'.* London. City University.
4. Freire, P., 1972. *'Pedagogy of the oppressed'.* Ringwood: Penguin.
5. Guetzkow, J., 2002. *'How the Arts Impact Communities: An introduction to the literature on arts impact studies'.* Working Paper #20, Summer 2002, Robert Hall, Princeton, NJ 08544-1013.
6. Merlin.
7. Sonn, CC. Drew, N. M., & Kasat, P., 2002. *Conceptualising community cultural development: The role of cultural planning in community change.* Perth: CAN WA.
8. Sonn, C.S. & Quayle, A.F., 2014. Stanziola *'Community Cultural Development for Social Change Developing Critical Praxis'.* Journal for Social Action in Counselling and Psychology. Volume 6, Number 1, Summer 2014.
9. Stanziola, J., 1999. *'Arts, government and community revitalisation'.* Ashgate: Aldershot, U.K., Brookfield, Vt. and Sydney.
10. Strom, E., 1999. *'Let's put on a show! Performing arts and urban civilisation in Newark, New Jersey'.* Pp 423-35 in Journal of Urban Affairs.

The Role of the Arts/Performing Arts in the...

11. Thomas, R.E., Rappaport, J., 1996. *'Art as community narrative: A resource for social change'*. In M. B. Lykes, R. Liem, A. Banuazizi, & M. Morris (Eds), 'Unmasking social inequalities: victims, voice and resistance (pp. 317-336). Philadelphia, PA: Temple University Press.

□

Diaspora and Nation-Building: An Indo-Mauritian Perspective

—Dr. Atanu Mohapatra
—Dr. Siba Sankar Mohanty

Introduction

Etymologically, the term 'Diaspora' refers to the 'dispersal', historically the dispersion of the Jews from their homeland. The etymological meaning of the term 'diaspora' is the scattering of the seeds. So, the seeds or the scattering of seeds carries a very positive dimension, as it suggests the germination. Though diaspora has carried different connotations in different phases of its history, yet 'diaspora' in the post-modern scenario carries a very positive connotation. Diaspora has not only played a significant role in the nation-building of the country of their residence, but also it has been contributing immensely to the development of their country of origin. Indian diaspora in Mauritius has played a very crucial role in shaping, nurturing and developing this beautiful country, and, at the same time, their contribution to India in different spheres has been quite significant. Hugh Tinker uses the symbol of Banyan tree to refer to the Indian diaspora. Banyan tree suggests deep rootedness as well as the spreading of the roots. Hugh Tinker cites Rabindranath Tagore who had said that "... India can live and grow by spreading abroad – not the political India, but the ideal India".

Indian diaspora in Mauritius has been the ambassador of India carrying and spreading the essence of India not only in Mauritius but also in different parts of the world.

Every country efforts to bring back the diasporic support in its nation-building process. All these efforts of a country draw social and patriotic linkages as a starting point and attempts to put in place Diaspora as a part of the country's national and institutional capacity-building efforts. It is also encouraging for the countries to note that Diaspora has a high contribution to the national growth process through the means such as remittances, knowledge.

Diaspora and Nation-Building

Ernest Renan defines nation as a soul, spiritual principle. Two aspects constitute the basic fabric of the spiritual principle. One in the past, that lies in the rich legacy of memories, sorrows, sufferings, past endeavours, sacrifices, devotion, heroic past and glory. The other lies in the present that focusses on the consent or common will to live together. In this sense, nations are necessary for guaranteeing and safeguarding the liberty and rights. Renan focusses on the aspirations of collective life of the people who aspire to live in a community. Victor Turner understands and perceives nation in terms of human relations, and he focusses on the human bonding without which there could be no society.

Imagination plays a very significant part in the formation and sustenance of a nation. Benedict Anderson argues that nation is an imagined community, and here it is important to note how it is imagined. Salman Rushdie in 'Imaginary Homelands' focusses on the imaginary in creating and reclaiming homelands. As he says, "Our physical alienation from India almost inevitably means that we will not be capable of reclaiming precisely the thing that was lost; that we will, in short, create fictions, not actual cities or villages, but invisible ones, imaginary homelands, Indias of the mind."

112 *Diaspora and Nation-Building*

Imagination has always been a very significant binding force in connecting India with its diaspora, and, in this context, the Indian diaspora of Mauritius and India. During the period of indentureship, imagination provided a kind of solace and certitude to the troubling and terrible lives of indentured labourers. Many of the people of younger generation have not been to India physically, yet they are connected with India through the imaginary India.

Vijay Misharefers to Laplanche and Pontalis who view that the term 'imaginary' is characterised by a residual narcissism, resemblance and homeomorphism. Vijay Mishra also refers to Slavoj Žižek who defines the imaginary as the state of 'identification with the image in which we appear likeable to ourselves, with the image representing 'what we would like to be'. As Vijay Mishra states, in a subsequent application of this theory to the nation itself, Žižek connects the idea of what he calls the 'Nation Thing' to its citizen's imaginary identification with it. The 'Nation qua Thing' comes out of a fantasy that a particular kind of enjoyment or property belongs to a particular group, and that particular group or community has the sole authority over the enjoyment of that property or group. In the colonial dispensation of Mauritius, Indians were not to be seen in the national narrative.

Role of Indian Diaspora in Mauritius in Nation-Building

About 70 percent of population of Mauritius are of Indian origin. Mauritius has been subjected to the changing of hands to many European colonisers ranging from Portuguese to Dutch, French and British. The arrival of many European colonisers and then the importation of people from different countries to Mauritius by the colonials had not only brought a serious change to the demographic, socio-cultural, economic, geographical and political spheres of Mauritius, but also it brought along with it cruelty, confusion and partisanship.

Diaspora and Nation-Building... 113

The arrival of Indians in Mauritius has not been an accident in history, rather as a part of the cruel ploy of the European colonial dispensation. Mostly, Indians in Mauritius arrived under the system of indentureship, a system which was based on unrealistic expectations offered to Indian labourers of comfortable and prosperous life which was not true. The following lines of Satendra Nandan, a famous Indo-Fijian poet, from his poem *Lines Across Black Waters*, encapsulates the whole of Indentureship:

Homeless I had come in search of paradise
This house of hell was now all mine.

Vijay Mishra discusses the routine of plantation life: din calekudārīrātnīndnahīmāve ('the hoe defines my days; insomnia my nights') sing women in the cane fields.

But in the gradual process by the dint of their hard work and determination, Indians overcame the drudgeries of indentureship, and have successfully established themselves in every sphere of Mauritian society.

Vijay Mishra studies Paul Gilroy, who, in his most famous book on diasporic history, *The Black Atlantic: Modernity and Double Consciousness*, juxtaposes the metaphors of 'root' and 'route'. Vijay Mishra argues that the 'root' metaphor reconstructs memorially a pristine, pure, uncontaminated homeland to which the first-generation immigrant dreamt of returning. Vijay Mishra in his *Ordering Naipaul: Indenture History and Diasporic Poetics*, locates the 'route' metaphor in two geographical spaces: one the ship and the other plantation barracks. Of the first, Mishra says: "The ship...is the first of the cultural units in which social relations are resisted and renegotiated. For the old, exclusivist Indian diaspora, the ship produced a site in which caste purities were largely lost (after all the crossing of the dark ocean, the *kalapani*, signified the loss of caste) as well as a new form of socialisation that went by the name of *Jahaji-Bhai* (ship brotherhood). Social interactions during these long sea voyages created a process

114   *Diaspora and Nation-Building*

that led to the remaking of cultural and ethnic identities, to a critical self-reflexivity of the kind missing from the stratified and less mobile institutions of the homeland." In the ship for the first time, people from different castes, religions, and regional and linguistic backgrounds met with each other, and developed a new form of socialisation. In the terrible plantation barracks and estates, Indian Indentured labourers, devoid of their backgrounds, were subjected to the same kind of tortures and horrendous life. Outside of their plantation life, Indians were also a subject of envy. So, Indians realised that it is their pan Indian identity, that is the belonging or having the root with the Mother India will provide them energy and motivation to struggle and succeed in a land which was hostile to them. We can read this attempt of Indians to organise themselves as the initial modulation of nation-building.

As a part of their ploy, the colonials were trying to divide the Indian community in terms of their religion, caste, region, language, etc., but due to the efforts of many Indo-Mauritians, and, later on, the great endeavours of one of the greatest sons of the land, and the father of modern Mauritius, Sir Seewoosagur Ramgoolam, the 'divide and rule' ploy of the colonials could not succeed. Indo-Mauritians held each other and worked hard, and due to their organisational skills, they have succeeded immensely in the political, economic and socio-cultural spheres of Mauritian society, and have contributed immensely to the development of Mauritius as a mature democracy and developed economy.

In the Mauritian context, when we talk about the national consciousness, nationalism, nation and nation-building, we must keep in mind that they are not simply a pre- or post-independence phenomenon, rather their roots can be traced to the period of indentureship and post-indentured days, where the Indian indentured labourers struggled a lot to survive in a strange land. In those turbulent days Indians

Diaspora and Nation-Building...   115

never forgot to maintain their cultures and communitarian life. The organisation of *kathas, satsangs, ramlila,* etc., not only brought about a spiritual solace in a turbulent life, but also helped them in organising themselves as a political community. Later, Indo-Mauritians became one of the pioneers of the freedom struggle of Mauritius.

Another interesting dimension to the nation-building of Mauritius is that the colonial encounter of Mauritius not only brought many European colonials to this land, but also Mauritius witnessed to the importation of people of different ethnicities from many countries (mostly as slaves and indentured labourers) of the world. Africans, Indians, Chinese, etc., were brought to Mauritius under the colonial dispensation to run the colonial economy of the Europeans. As diaspora, these groups maintained a kind of communication linkage with their homelands primarily through the retention of cultural practices and imaginary creation of homelands. But, most importantly, many diaspora groups have come together and joined hands to the building of a consolidated nation, that is Mauritius. Indeed, the nation-building of Mauritius bears ample testimony to how diasporas become a nation. What is significant here is that the preservation of diasporic sensibilities helps and enables in consolidating the nation.

When we analyse a society with various socio-cultural groups or entities, issues and notion identity becomes very important. Stuart Hall theorises two ways of reflecting on the cultural identity – firstly, identity as understood as a collective, shared history among individuals affiliated by race or ethnicity and from that perspective, identity is fixed or stable, and secondly, identity understood as unstable, metamorphic and even contradictory – an identity marked by multiple points of similarities and differences. From this second perspective, identity is viewed as not an accomplished fact. Identity is a production which is never complete, and it

116 *Diaspora and Nation-Building*

is always in process. The identity of the Indo-Mauritians can be understood from these two perspectives. Indo-Mauritians have retained a kind of collective Indian identity, at the same time, their identity have been negotiated and renegotiated in the interaction with the outer Mauritian society. The revitalisation of their diasporic sensibilities is strengthened through their connectedness with their roots.

Chérif Saloum Diatta in her doctoral study uses the symbol of 'pilau' to focus on the unity of the Trinidian nation. Diatta says that 'pilau' is a national dish that symbolises the unity of the Trinidadian nation. This dish is made of a mixture of sweetened rice, meat and vegetables. As Diatta says, for Harney, the national symbolism of 'pilau' is significant because "the Chinese, Spanish, Africans and Indians all claim they brought the recipe to the island". However, he argues that constructing the Trinidadian nation should go beyond just cooking of the 'pilau'. It should incorporate the examination of "who cooks, who eats, and who does neither". This view of nationalism includes all social segments – ethnic, class and gender categories into the definition of Trinidadian national space. So, it is the societal pluralism that defines the Mauritian nation.

India and its Diaspora Engagement: Pre-Independence Era to the Present-day Scenario

During the period of European colonialism, Indians were transported to different countries of the world as Indentured labourers or contract labourers. Most of them were the British citizens of India. Since India was not independent at that time, and India was not its destiny maker, India could not do anything for its children who were forced to leave their motherland due to the colonial dispensation. But Indian leaders made an emotional appeal to the overseas Indians underlining the love and affection for them. This can be best captured in these lines of Jawaharlal Nehru. On

Diaspora and Nation-Building... 117

March 18, 1946, while addressing a predominantly Indian gathering in Singapore, he said, "India cannot forget her sons and daughters overseas. Although India cannot defend her children overseas today, the time is soon coming when her arm will be long enough to protect them." (Sharma 2013).

Overseas Indians were very much keen on the developments in India. Gopal Krishna Gokhale was very much concerned about the betterment of overseas Indians especially of the indentured labourers. He was one of the pioneers of the fight against the abolition of Indentureship. Mahatma Gandhi had the first-hand knowledge and experience of being 'coolie Indians'. C.F. Andrews, the friend of the poor (also known as Deena Bandhu), had seen the terrible and drudging living conditions of Indentured labourers and their younger generations. So, with the fight of the many Indian nationalists and civil society organisations, Indentureship came to an end in 1920.

In the Pre-Independence era, freedom fighters of India had a great concern for the overseas Indians, and they always wanted the betterment of the Indians living so far away from India. On the other end, overseas Indians had always looked upon India as a source of solace and inspiration. Sir Seewoosagur Ramgoolam and other Indo-Mauritians had greatly supported the cause of India's independence. Cola Reinzi, an Indo-Trinidadian, a student leader was generating public opinion in England for the independence of India in the 1930s, when Mahatma Gandhi had gone to England for the Round Table Conference. Overseas Indians in their respective countries in different ways supported the cause of India's independence and generated public opinion for it. They were looking at this as their own independence.

Finally, India got its independence. The first Prime Minister of India Jawaharlal Nehru who had once said that once India becomes independent and makes its own destiny, India won't forget its children leaving outside of India, now

118 *Diaspora and Nation-Building*

after independence in the Constituent Assembly on 8 March, 1948, he told:

"Now these Indians abroad, what are they? Are they Indian citizens – are they going to be citizens of India or not? If they are not, then our interest in them becomes cultural, humanitarian and not political. ... For instance, take the Indians in Fiji or Mauritius. Are they going to retain their nationality, or will they become Fijian nationals or Mauritians? The same question arises in regard to Burma and Ceylon. It is a difficult question. This House gets mixed up. It wants to treat them as Indians, and with the same breath, it wants a complete franchise for them in the countries where they are living" (Lal 2006).

Nehru also asked the overseas Indians to integrate in their host countries and not to spoil the fair name of India abroad. Overseas Indians who were looking upon the independence of India with so much of hope and aspirations were heart-broken by these developments and statements. They had also to face the brunt of the local communities.

During the Indo-Chinese War in 1962, India welcomed contributions and support of the overseas Indians. When questioned on this, Nehru told a foreign journalist, "Indians overseas have dual loyalty, one to their country of adoption and other to their country of origin" (Gupta 1974). So, a kind of duality was to be marked in India's foreign policy towards its diaspora from the Nehruvian era till the 1991 when India had to encounter the serious foreign debt crisis. Overseas Indians helped India during this period and the liberalisation of the Indian economy provided a platform to the overseas Indians to invest in the economy of India. But the marking point in India's engagement with its diaspora can be marked during the Vajpayee government. Under the Vajpayee government, a high-level committee under the chairmanship of L.M. Singhvi was formed to make systematic study of the overseas Indians living in different parts of the

Diaspora and Nation-Building... 119

world. The committee for the first time made a detailed study of the overseas Indians and submitted a report which goes by the name of High-Level Committee Report of Indian Diaspora or Singhvi Committee Report. The committee made certain recommendations, like Pravasi Bharatiya Divas, Pravsi Bharatiya Samman, dual citizenship, etc. Government of India accepted most of its recommendations and contemplated on others. The subsequent governments followed the same kind of policies of the Vajapayee government. The Indian diaspora is very much dear to the heart of the present Prime Minister, Shri Narendra Modi. Whichever foreign country he goes, he addresses the diasporic community there. Prime Minister Modi has been focussing on the diaspora as a significant strategic asset for India. He has created many avenues where the diasporic expertise, knowledge, innovation, enterprise and all kinds of assets and resources are tapped for the development of India and the diaspora.

Government of India has undertaken many programmes for the Indian diaspora, such as PIO Card, Know India Programme (KIP), Study India Programme (SIP), Scholarship Programmes for Diaspora Children (SPDC), Indian Community Welfare Fund (ICWF), Mahatma Gandhi Pravasi Suraksha Yojana (MGPSY) and many more others. Indian diaspora can take benefit of these programmes.

Diaspora and Development: An Indian Perspective

Historically, diaspora contributes for the establishment of small, micro, medium, and large enterprises and entrepreneurship. But, in most of the cases of small and micro enterprises, operations are conducted by the family members who do not have requisite managerial competencies, financial management capabilities and supply chain. In a wider perspective, the diaspora also contributes for value-chain extensions. The diasporic community is active in establishing small businesses, such as agriculture,

120   *Diaspora and Nation-Building*

export-import, transportation, artisan, brick manufacturing, masonry and carpentry. Such activities have implications for youth employment and income generation – both in the ancestral and host land.

The most significant means of diasporic nation-building generally comes through individual remittances, which is followed by hometown associations, charitable initiatives, etc., that directly affect capacity-building, economic development and poverty reduction. Governments of migrant-sending and receiving countries, international agencies, and academics are now paying vital attention and interest for the development of relationship between diasporas and the development. Remittances by the migrants have turned as important as official development assistance (ODA). Remittances, in nature, are more stable than capital inflows and household remittances can contribute more, which lays the foundation for effective poverty reduction measures, having large-scale implications and long-lasting solutions. Remittances ensure benefits through various levels. The diasporic community prefers to invest in their ancestral or own countries in establishing small businesses with the assumption that they might one day come back and would have a source of income at their living. Such investments include transfer of technology, purchase of land and assets, enhancement of skills, and relatively modernised approach to management, regional markets and cross-border trade.

At the household level, recipients of remittances in host countries, as seen in the African countries, found to have higher levels of savings than those who were not receiving money from abroad. For example, about 10-20% of the US$ 40 billion remittance flows to Africa is saved or invested. Moreover, evidence shows that a 10 % increase in official international remittances as a share of Gross Domestic Product (GDP) leads to a 2.9% decline in the poverty reduction in Africa. Remittances also support families during

Diaspora and Nation-Building...   121

national issues and crisis such as when the regular salaries and wages are often interrupted.

In India, there are some obvious and niche areas to be analysed, so that the broad contours of Indian diaspora could be better reflected.

- Is there a link between diaspora, remittance and development?
- What kind of role does the Indian diaspora play in the development of the host countries?
- What role the Indian diaspora can play in the development of their ancestral land – India?
- What are the strategies the Indian government is using to deal with its diasporic community?
- What are the lessons that could be learnt from the Indian model of engagement?

India has the facilities for attracting highly skilled professionals of its diasporic community to its land. The high-quality research environments, education and incentives provide plethora of opportunities for the development of human resources. Moreover, establishment of subsidiaries, multi-nationals and of joint ventures between multi-nationals of the host country and Indian firms will enhance the incentives and the spirit of fraternity. India in 1998 launched and sold $4.2 billion worth of 5-year bonds targeting the Diaspora within a period of two weeks, shortly after India's second nuclear tests in 1998. Significantly, the success of this bond issuance prompted the government to issue another bond in 2000 under the scheme of India Millennium Deposits, which raised an additional worth of 5.5 billion dollars. The scheme provided incentives such as an interest rate of two percent higher in dollar terms than the U.S. bond market, option to redeem in U.S. dollars, German marks, and the bond was guaranteed by the State Bank of India, exempted from Indian taxes. Moreover, India launched these bonds, which were available to the non-resident Indians, with intensive marketing campaigns at the international level.

An important field gaining importance today includes reducing brain drain in developing countries. Hence, innovative national and international programmes for "tapping the diaspora" have been put in place, so that India can have the opportunity of expatriate expertise, knowledge, and experience, along with external networks for trade, communications and technological advancement. The Skill India programme and Make in India programme, like all other innovative and pragmatic steps by the Narendra Modi government, make a great sense for bonding Indian diaspora with India. The program will support thousands of emigrant nationals with professional expertise to come to their country of origin – India and work for mutual advantage.

According to the World Bank, remittances can reduce recipient household poverty; increase of investment in health, education and other productive activities; reduction of child labour and increase of entrepreneurship. The assumption that remittances have a positive effect on development is, since underdevelopment, emigration and remittances are correlated in nature. The social rate of return to a unit of Diaspora investments generally higher than that of foreign direct investment from non-Diaspora sources. According to the Reserve Bank of India (RBI) remittances to India reached US$46.4 billion for fiscal year (FY) 2008-09 up from US$2.1 billion in FY 1990-91. The World Bank data shows a dramatic increase of almost 162% in the remittance that India receives from overseas Indians over the last eight years. While India received nearly $21 billion from overseas Indians in 2003, the figure jumped to $64 billion in 2011. It also revealed that India received the highest remittance, followed by other countries in the world.

Beyond remittances, diasporas contribute to the economic development of their country of origin through

Diaspora and Nation-Building... 123

Foreign Direct Investment (FDI) and transnational entrepreneurship, including support for entrepreneurs and small businesses in the country of origin. Mauritius is one of the largest contributors to FDI in India. This indicates that there is a unique combination of ownership advantages and joint ventures to forecast new developments in the country of origin – India and, thus, there is a difference between diaspora involvement in the development of their ancestral land and non-diaspora FDI. The diaspora investments may be guided not only by profit motives, but also by long-run considerations of establishing a base in the countries of their origin. They are likely to be better informed on the capabilities and requirements of domestic labour and the sort of training local labour requires. Many times, the factors which influenced the diaspora to migrate from their land of origin influence the extent of their involvement and contribution to the development of their countries of origin. There is a favorable and positive effect as migrants may return after a while, embodying a brain grain, and skilled migrants may post remittances. The constructive contributions of diasporas to development in their country of origin include transfer of acquired knowledge. The knowledge transfer includes higher education and specialised skills. The skilled diaspora is most commonly defined phenomenon where the qualification and possession of a tertiary degree or extensive specialised work experience counts. The diaspora is a great source and means of transfer of technical skill and knowledge in the form of 'brain gain' and 'brain circulation'. The diaspora members can act as important interlocutors between the technology and country of origin, where the knowledge exchange is concerned. They may contribute through permanent repatriation, short-term or virtual return. Sometimes, the most important contribution the diaspora may bring to the country of origin is belief in the possibility of change, entrepreneurship and

124 *Diaspora and Nation-Building*

innovation. This can be best explained through the post-1991 economic reform and FDI policies to attract investment also from the diaspora.

Conclusion

To fulfill its broader objective of remittance and FDI, the Indian government has taken the following measures:

- The Overseas Indian Facilitation Centre (OIFC), a not for profit trust, in partnership with the Confederation of Indian Industry (CII), serve as a one stop shop for economic engagement, investment and business.
- The India Development Foundation (IDF), a non-profit trust, serves as a credible single window to facilitate diaspora philanthropy and lead overseas Indian philanthropic capital into India's social development effort.
- The India Centre for Migration (ICM), a not-for-profit society, serves as a strategic 'think-tank' on matters relating to overseas employment markets for Indians and overseas Indian workers.
- The Global Indian Network of Knowledge (Global INK), a robust electronic platform, facilitates transfer of knowledge with the objective of leveraging skills and expertise.
- Tax incentives such as reduced customs duty regime.
- Providing opportunities for the Overseas Indians who are returning to India to stay up to three years after return.
- Ensuring portable benefits through the provision of SSAs (Social Security Agreements). Pensionary which includes Indian workers and professionals working overseas are both portable and can be totalised in countries where SSAs have been executed.

Diaspora and Nation-Building... 125

As we know that Indo-Mauritians are highly industrious and enterprising people, they can take out the best from the various initiatives and programmes undertaken by the Government of India. At the same time, the relationship between India and its diaspora should not be solely based on economic investment. More and more interactions should be made at the socio-cultural level. Though the Government of India's approach of engaging the diaspora in the developmental process has been quite pro-active in the recent years, yet the GOI needs to do more to strengthen and carry forward the relationship to a greater level.

To conclude, we may say that by the dint of their hard work, determination and progressive attitude Indo-Mauritians have played a very pivotal role in the building of Mauritius as such a vibrant nation, and, at the same time, their contribution to India in different spheres is quite noteworthy. The hard work and success story of the Indo-Mauritians can best be captured in the following lines of the famous Indo-Mauritian poet, Vishwamitra Ganga Ashutosh:

> *No Gold did they find*
> *Underneath any stone they*
> *Touched and turned, yet*
> *Every stone they touched*
> *Into solid gold they turned*

Notes and References

1. Alwyn Didar Singh, 2012, *Working with the Diaspora for Development Policy Perspectives from India,* CARIM-India RR 2012/25, European University Institute.

2. Anderson, Benedict (1982), *Imagined Communities Reflections on the Origin and Rise of Nationalism*, London: Verso.

3. Anyanwu, J.C., and A.E.O. Erhijakpor. 2010. Do International Remittances Affect Poverty in Africa? African Development Review, 22 (1): 51-91.

4. Brinkerhoff, Jennifer M. (ed.) (2008) *Diaspora and*

126   *Diaspora and Nation-Building*

Development: Exploring the Potential, Lynne Rienner Publishers, Boulder, London.

5. Diatta, Chérif Saloum (2015), *Nation and Diaspora Caribbean Identities and Community Politics in the Fiction of Earl Lovelace*, Ph.D. Thesis, New Orleans: Tulane University.

6. Gamlen, Alan (2006), Diaspora Engagement Policies: What are They, and What Kind of States Use Them? University of Oxford, Centre on Migration Policy and Society, *Working Paper no. 32.*

7. Gilroy, Paul (1993), *The Black Atlantic: Modernity and Double Consciousness*, Cambridge, Mass.: Harvard University Press. Quoted in Vijay Mishra (2007), *The Literature of the Indian Diaspora Theorising the Diasporic Imaginary*, New York: Routledge.

8. Government of India (GOI) (2000), Report of the High Level Committee on the Indian Diaspora, Ministry of External Affairs, New Delhi.

9. Gupta, Anirudha (1974), 'Ugandan Asians, Britain, India and the Commonwealth', *African Affairs*, 73 (292): 312-324, [Online: web] Accessed 25 June 2018, URL: www.jstor.com.

10. Hall, Stuart (2003), 'Cultural Identity and Diaspora', in Jana Evans Braziel and Anita Mannur (eds.), *Theorising Diaspora A Reader*, Malden: Blackwell Publishing Ltd.

11. Harney, Stefano (1969), *Nationalism and Identity: Culture and the Imagination in a Caribbean Diaspora*, London & New Jersey: Zed Books. Quoted in Chérif Saloum Diatta (2015), *Nation and Diaspora Caribbean Identities and Community Politics in the Fiction of Earl Lovelace*, Ph.D. Thesis, New Orleans: Tulane University.

12. Lal, Brij V. (2006) (ed.), *The Encyclopedia of the Indian Diaspora*, Singapore: Editions Didier Millet.

13. Laplanche, J. and Pontalis, J.-B. (1980) *The Language of Psycho-analysis*, trans. Donald Nicholson-Smith, intr. Daniel Lagache, London: The Hogarth Press. Quoted in Vijay Mishra (2007), *The Literature of the Indian Diaspora*

Diaspora and Nation-Building... 127

Theorising the diasporic imaginary, New York: Routledge.

14. Mishra, Vijay (2007), *The Literature of the Indian Diaspora Theorising the Diasporic Imaginary*, New York: Routledge.

15. Newland, K., and E. Patrick: 'Beyond Remittances: the Role of Diaspora in Poverty Reductions in their Countries of Origin', Migration Policy Institute, Washington D.C., USA, July 2004.

16. Ozden, Caolar and Schiff, Maurice (eds.) (2005) *International Migration, Remittances and the Brain Drain*, Washington, DC: World Bank.

17. Rapoport, Hillel (2008), Brain Drain and Development: An Overview Presented to the AFD, Workshop on Migration and Human Capital Development, Paris, June 30, 2008.

18. Renan, Ernest (1990), 'What is a nation', in Homi Bhabha (ed.), *Nation and Narration*, London: Routledge.

19. Rushdie, Salman (1991), *Imaginary Homelands Essays and Criticism, 1981-1991*, London: Vintage Books.

20. Sharma, J.C. (Dec 03, 2013), 'India's Foreign Policy, National Security & Development', Distinguished Lectures, Ministry of External Affairs, Government of India, [Online: web] Accessed 25 June 2018, URL: http://www.mea.gov.in/foreign-policy.htm.

21. Somini Sengupta, 'India Taps Into Its Diaspora', *New York Times*, 19 Aug 1998.

22. Steven Vertovec, 2005, Centre on Migration, Policy and Society, Working Paper No. 13.

23. The Role of the Diaspora in Nation-Building: Lessons for Fragile and Post-Conflict Countries in Africa, African Development Bank.

24. Tinker, Hugh (1977), *The Banyan Tree: Overseas Emigrants from India, Pakistan and Bangladesh*, Oxford: Oxford University Press.

25. Turner, Victor (1969), *The Ritual Process: Structure and Anti-Structure*, Chicago: Aldine Pub. Co. Quoted in Chérif Saloum Diatta (2015), *Nation and Diaspora Caribbean Identities and Community Politics in the Fiction of Earl Lovelace*, Ph.D. Thesis, New Orleans: Tulane University.

128   *Diaspora and Nation-Building*

26. World Bank (2012), Migration and Development Brief.
27. Žižek, Slavoj (1989), *The Sublime Object of Ideology*, London: Verso. Quoted in Vijay Mishra (2007), *The Literature of the Indian Diaspora Theorising the Diasporic Imaginary*, New York: Routledge.

□

Indian Diaspora and Culture on the French Territory Reunion

—Dr. Jean-Régis Ramsamy

In 1986, even before the installation of an Indian Consulate in La Reunion, I wrote to the Ministry of Foreign Affairs asking for a greater support to our struggle into developing the Indian culture in this French island. I am only reminding myself of the work already started by several elders.

With the help of friends, we created three local associations: the Office for Diaspora (founded by Professor A.K. Dubey, Jawaharlal Nehru University (JNU), the Global Organisation of People of Indian Origin (GOPIO) Saint-Denis and the Indian Diaspora Council (IDC) (created by Ashook Ramsaran, former president of GOPIO.

La Reunion History in a Few Lines

La Reunion is a French territory and the people of Indian origin represent at least 35% of the total population. Most of the People of Indian Origin (PIOs) are from Tamil Nadu. Hinduism is the second most important religion on the island. Dina Margabin was the name given by the pioneers who discovered it in the 16th century and was an important part of the Mascarenhas archipelago. This island is 2,512 km^2 and in recent decades, has grown with each eruption.

130 *Diaspora and Nation-Building*

In the official documentation, the Europeans (the Portuguese Pedro de Mascarenhas) had discovered the island. The Africans, known locally as Cafres, were involved in trading and agriculture and started with the plantations of coffee. From Madagascar (Fort-Dauphin) came the first settlers of Reunion in 1665, along with Etienne Regnault (the first governor of La Reunion). When the Indians arrived on the island, it was known as Isle Bourbon.

At the beginning of the 19th century, the big plantation owners became sure that sugar cane would be the best agricultural crop for trading. Thus, they conspicuously turned to India for the supply of labour. India was known to them as a place of human and cultural exchange.

From 1820 to 1917, about 1,20,000 Indian workers were brought to Reunion, a place named 'Birboon' in their tongue. They came mainly from southern India and also from Gujarat, Bihar and Bengal. Unfortunately, the descendants were not able to preserve the mother tongue of their ancestors. On the other hand, they remarkably adapted themselves to the French island, whilst still having strong Indian culture and traditions. Some descendants of indentured workers have even become landowners, some major political figures and others became important social leaders. The Reunionese of Indian origin (ROI) managed to stamp their mark on the development of the island of Reunion. The sugar cane industry became the main reason for the arrival of an intensive Indian labour force.

Culture of the La Reunion

The people of this French island are very close to their history. During the sole month of July 2018, about 150 people walked through fire, a ceremony also known as the semblani, in order to respect and honour their ancestors. Local TV networks broadcasted the pious event throughout the island.

In 2011, when the GOPIO set up a monument to Coolies in Kolkata, I was present there. After such an event, I sent a

Indian Diaspora and Culture on... 131

message to Mr. Ashok Ramsaran, former president of GOPIO, to tell him that after a north Indian monument, there should also be a monument in southern part of India. He concurred and suggested that he was keen to see if some kind of monument could be erected in La Reunion also. Thus, in 2014, a new Indian Culture Centre was built in La Reunion. To inaugurate the centre, Dr. Mahesh Sharma, Minister of Tourism, Culture and Civil Aviation, was the chief guest. This symbolised the strengthening of cultural and economic ties between La Reunion and India.

Egata Patché

Despite all these cultural activities, we must recognise that we have weaknesses. Mr. Abady Egata-Patché is part of the group of people, who think in analysing the past to the betterment of the future. According to him, our ancestors suffered a lot of pain with the indentured servitude. He pleads for recognition of ancestors nationally and internationally.

Since the last 5 years, this man engaged himself in a new fight to prove that indentured labour (or coolie system, or Girmitya) was a kind of new form of slavery. In Hugh Tinker book, there are detailed explanations about this new form of slavery. We believe in Mr. Egata-Patché's words and we are launching a book, written in French for now, which will be translated later.

Mr. Egata-Patché wants to go to an international court, such as The Hague, to show the world the real face of coolie-trade or struggles of the indentured labours as observed in La Reunion Island. He wants to prove that the people are still subjected to the consequences of the coolie-trade or the migration of indentured labours within La Reunion. This may be different in Mauritius as our history differs.

OCI Card Issue

In the island, there are about a thousand depositories of

132 *Diaspora and Nation-Building*

the Overseas Citizenship (OCI) of India, out of a total of some 300,000 Reunionese of Indian origins. From about a thousand depositories of the Overseas Citizenship of India (OCI) cards there are a total of some 300,000 ROIs. My responsibility is to point out the events on the topic of Indo Reunionese Diaspora.

The people in the island wish to see stronger relationship with India. As a consequence, PIO in La Reunion finds it difficult to understand why the new OCI card is not extended up to the fifth generation. The reason why the new accord is not extended to their land is unknown.

People think that if PIOs in La Reunion are really part of the Indian diaspora, they should have the same rights. Around 50 files of OCI cards for locals are held up for some reasons or other reasons, even though there is a dedicated Indian consulate. PIOs in La Reunion are forced to prove their grandparents' identity. It is a real issue.

Anyways, our Indian diaspora also has a lot of strong points. First, there is an Indian consulate for thirty years now and it has moved to a new, more convenient location, helping the people to gain access to its facilities. Second, recently, the Indian Minister of Foreign Affairs came to visit the island and strengthening the relationship between La Reunion and India. Third, UNESCO has set up coordinated monuments as an international recognition of migrant workers all around the Indian Ocean, including in La Reunion Island.

It is, common understanding that the economy needs to grow and develop and over the decades, the Indian diaspora have helped build the country a great deal. Along with economic development of the island, the Indian diaspora has also provided a robust cultural identity.

About Culture in Reunion Island

Local Creole language is reminiscent of the old 17th century French. It also exhibits some English and Dutch words,

Indian Diaspora and Culture on... 133

and, of course, Malagasy words. Tamil and Hindi words, such as Rougail, Tangol, Ajoupa and Langouti are also included. These words are now so familiar to the Reunionese public that they don't even know these are foreign words. They find their roots in Southern India. Other words such as Kabay, digdig, mingled, etc., remind us of the Hindi influence on the local language.

Besides, some buildings have inscriptions in Tamil, probably indicating the site's name (Goddess Shakti Mariamman), as well as its benefactors' names. More fragments with Tamil inscriptions were located in various parts of the island.

Indians from Guadeloupe, Martinique and La Reunion mostly came from South India, especially from Tamil Nadu. Their ancestors' language has survived through the practice of religious rituals. From Kavadi to the fire-walking ceremony, most rituals are connected to the goddess Mariamman. All these religious ceremonies helped keep alive the transmission of Tamil, their forefather's mother tongue. This is why, nowadays, there is a renewed interest for learning the Tamil language, as it is seen as a way to reassert their Indian identity.

On the cultural and religious aspects, it is not necessary to look very far. ROUs celebrate Indian festivals with zeal. It is happy to know that Reunion Island has over 25,000 people attending Diwalî celebrations in each local region of the island during the months of October-November every year. Over the past 50 years, this celebration has become the flagship or the torch-bearer in popularising the Indian cultural heritage on the island. The Pongol Sankranti (originated from Tamil Nadu) is still celebrated in temples or in homes with family members. The kavady (Tamil festival to Subramanian, son of Shiva) is the subject of a large ritual, as well as the fire-walking ceremony. I said that we lost our Indian heritage in terms of languages, but let me tell you that a revival does

134 *Diaspora and Nation-Building*

exist. People do try to learn Tamil. They need to be closer with their Hinduism. Young people, who have very high grades in school, don't accept priest as Gurukkal. There is a sense of detachment of culture.

About Diaspora

The concept of Girmitya practically does not appear in the papers about Indian immigration in Reunion Island. In the French language, the term used is 'engagisme', which means the Indian worker commits himself, and in English, they use the words 'indentured labours' or 'Coolie-trade' to translate the phenomenon. In New Delhi, during the last Pravasi Bharatiya Divas (PBD) at the Ministry of External Affairs held in January 2016, scholars had the opportunity to underline the importance of this historical period. In the case of Reunion Island, the term 'Malabar/Malabare' benefits from an old legitimacy.

Ties with Mauritius

Strengthening cultural relations between Mauritius and Reunion should produce impact in the social field and in the economy of both islands as well. It's my proper vision of my country, La Reunion, India and Mauritius, working side by side, helping one another. Mauritius is an independent country, whereas ReUnion is an overseas territory of France. I have to specify: Nobody speaks English in my country, our ancestors who left India, never spoke English, Tamil, Hindi or any Indian language. My communication is not a comparison between Mauritius, La Reunion and India. The purpose is only to highlight some common issues of both the islands.

Achievements

Our question is – in which manner did the Indian Diaspora influence the development of culture in Reunion Island? There is Fanny, poet Laucassade's mother, who owned two slaves,

Indian Diaspora and Culture on... 135

one being a Bengali, and Leconte de Lisle Adam who narrated his love for India in 'The Manchy' while introducing his two Telenga workers. Finally, during a short trip to the colony, Beaudelaire was caught under the spell of Indian ladies, a memory he recalls in his Fleurs du Mal, with the poem The Malabaraise (1840). We temporarily conclude this review of the presence of Indians in Reunion Island (through words and actions), with the entry of the word 'curry' (or 'kari') in the French Larousse Dictionary (2016).

People of Indian origin in Reunion also contributed to the development of Diasporas' literature. Mauritius and Reunion have contributed a lot to French literature, and the contributions have been mostly from Indian settlers.

There is no question of engaging in an inventory of products that relate to India, but simply to highlight some lines that appear and mark the contributions of Indians in the Island's cultural and social history. The island has adapted itself to rice, the national dish, which is, undoubtedly, the contribution of the Indian Indentured labourers. It is true that locally the islanders preferred bread over rice, but it remains the special dish when inviting a guest. This certainly exemplifies the importance of rice on the island way of life. We also have, apart from rice, spices like curry (a form of curry), and different varieties of vegetables that are the contribution of Indians to the islands. Every locality has its own vegetable market on different days, which can be traced back from the times of the indentured labourers. It may be noted that products as yams, maize or other starchy foods were consumed by slaves but now have been disappeared.

Finally, the Bollywood phenomenon encountered a fertile ground in Reunion Island. Many young people identified with the explosion of Indian fashion, seeing a homecoming through many Indian channels like Zee TV and many more. Besides, the elegant Shahrukh Khan is popularly remembered thanks to his concert on the island and by promising to make movies on the island as the islanders were emotionally attached to the Bollywood icons. I am hopeful that, in future, India will continue to influence the development of Reunion island. I remember, five years ago, our council, Region Reunion started to talk with Indian Oil. It is a good beginning.

I shall conclude to remember this quote, *the sun never set on the Indian Diaspora.*

□

Indian Diaspora: Contribution of Diaspora in Nation-Building

—*Rajesh Gogna*

Introduction: An Identity Issue

Our identities as individuals are like our souls without which the individual is lifeless. Like a tree, affixed to the ground by its roots, our identities give us a foundation to shape ourselves in a manner which projects and reflects our shared past, present and future with other human beings, with whom we share a connection because of our common culture, religion, language and traditions. This connection provides us with the tools to identity ourselves in this big world and helps us survive.

The Indian identity is based on the shared tradition, language and religion practised by the people of India. This identity gave them the hope and strength to venture out from their place of birth to faraway and distant lands in search of new opportunities and adventure. This search, at times, was undertaken voluntarily and, at times, involuntarily. However, it led to the spread and rise of the Indian community globally. This journey took them to new places like the Reunion Islands, Mauritius, Malaysia, Fiji, Africa and the Caribbean, etc. In their new homes, the Indian community continued to practise their religion, culture and speak their native language. This has allowed them to enrich not only their lives

138   *Diaspora and Nation-Building*

but also add to the existing way of life in their new homes in a positive way.

The Indian identity, very much cherished by the first-generation Indian immigrants has, in the subsequent years, decades and centuries, taken a backseat. It has led to the assimilation of the Indian identity with that of the indigenous population or a total loss of the Indian identity. This has created a flower without its smell, i.e., a thing without essence. I am reminded of a quote by the popular American fiction writer, H.P. Lovecraft, "No death, no doom, no anguish can arouse the surpassing despair which flows from a loss of identity." In the present times, the Indian diaspora is living in a dilemma; they are neither the citizens of the countries of their adoption (except for the name sake) nor the citizens of India. In the countries of their adoption, they are not treated as first-class citizens as evident from examples in countries like Malaysia, Fiji, Mauritius and Reunion Islands. For example, in Seychelles, Indian culture has lived along with other cultures for long, but is gradually giving way to a mixed culture, which retains more of French customs, habit and common law. Indian community in Seychelles in course of their assimilation process has lost its language. Also the Indian community has adopted French cuisine and ways and manners. Likewise, in Mauritius, the Indian community has accommodated more and more of French traditions and have let slip their own Indian heritage.

The situation is much better in comparison to the Reunion Islands, where Indian immigrants are today heavily involved in the French culture. If we neglect their physical characteristics and patronymics, they are simply French citizens, like other members of this multicultural society. This foregoing of identity is involuntary and unfortunate, but in places like Malaysia, the Indian community is systematically being deprived of its identity ever since the shift to a Malay hegemonic model of politics in the aftermath of the 1969

Indian Diaspora: Contribution of... 139

ethnic riots. In other places like Fiji, though the Indian identity is still intact, in recent times, it has come under threat because of political and ethnic tensions.

The identity issue for the Indian diaspora is a very real and grave one and can only be tackled with the help from within and outside the Indian community in a couple of different ways. Firstly, self-realisation of the importance among the Indian community about their Indian identity passed on from their forefathers. Secondly, assistance from the governments of their adopted nations to provide them the backing and the help to preserve their culture, tradition and language and also from international institutions to help the Indian community wherever and whenever the community has come under threat, so as to help them maintain and continue their basis of existence.

From Identity to Human Rights: A Challenge

The challenges faced by the Indian community are not singular in nature. The identity issue underlines or has, in turn, led to a bigger problem, that is, abrogation of Human Rights of the Indian community in their respective adopted countries. As the Indian diaspora lost their identities, they lose their sense of community and roots, which, in turn, makes them easy targets of marginalisation at the hands of either a despotic government or a dominant indigenous group, either of which don't want to share the pie of opportunity and growth in their respective governments, economic institutions, education sector, etc., with the 'outsiders'. This is evident from various instances of exploitation and subjugation experienced by the Indian community.

In Fiji, Indo-Fijians comprise the second largest ethnic group (37 per cent of the population) and are culturally and economically diverse. More than 90 percent are descendants of indentured labourers and the remainders are descendants of free migrant. A small number of Indo-Fijians can be defined

140 *Diaspora and Nation-Building*

as wealthy or engaged in business enterprises, but the majority of Indo-Fijians are workers and peasant farmers, and also include the poorest of the poor in the country. Indo-Fijian tenant farmers rely on leased agricultural land and, since 1999, many of these leases have not been renewed, or are at the point of expiration, resulting in the lease-holders being displaced. As a result, Indo-Fijians are among the largest category of landless people in Fiji. This is a source of anxiety and hardship as they often have no other means of sustenance, and feel a real sense of political marginalisation. As a group, there has been a high degree of stress since the coups of 1987 and 2000 particularly after the events of 2000, in which many Indo-Fijians were beaten up and raped, and their property looted and burnt. The Indian community there has been traumatised.[1]

In Malaysia, Indians constitute about eight percent of the population. The shift from an ethnic elite cooperation mechanism to a Malay hegemonic model of politics in the aftermath of the 1969 ethnic riots has been particularly hard on numerically weaker ethnic communities in the country. Amid its social and economic marginalisation, the Indian community has faced serious challenges in the last three decades due to major changes in the plantation sector. As the country progressed, recording impressive economic growth rates from the 1980s, the largely Indian plantation resident communities were left behind, as well as becoming victims to the overall national development. More than three hundred thousand poor Indian workers have been displaced after the plantations were acquired for property and township development over the years. When evicted from the plantations, these people not only lost their jobs, but, more importantly, housing, basic amenities and socio-cultural facilities built up over decades. Despite the very large number of people involved in this involuntary stream of migration from rural plantation areas to urban areas, little or nothing was

Indian Diaspora: Contribution of... 141

done by the authorities to provide skills training in order to resettle these communities in more sustainable and improved livelihoods. Thus, the government's discriminatory policies and the poor living conditions of the displaced community contributed to a situation where many Indian youths have turned to illegal activities to sustain themselves.

The current affirmative action program in Malaysia, officially called the 'Bumiputera' policy—Bumiputera means 'sons of the soil'—has led to a deeply fractured nation and perpetual ethnic tensions. This gives Malays and other indigenous groupings a wide range of government help, including easy entry to universities, cheap business loans, scholarships, public service jobs, employment quotas in private sector jobs, and special government tenders. Indians are relegated to second-class citizenship and are no longer able to rely on government help or attend institutions of higher learning due to the quota system.

Besides economic and political discrimination, religious persecution has been a formidable source of marginalisation for the people of Indian origin in Malaysia. According to various sources, religious tensions have increased following an acceleration of the demolition of Hindu temples by local governments to make way for development projects. Many Hindu temples and shrines throughout the country have been destroyed, including temples in Kuala Lumpur and in the states of Selangor and Negeri Sembilan. As reported in an article by the Associated Press (AP), the lobby group Hindu Rights Action Force (Hindraf) claimed that "more than 70 Hindu temples were razed or threatened with such action in 2006". In the last couple of years, the growing religious intolerance and Islamic conservatism has heightened the sense of insecurity among minorities, especially in Indian Hindus.[2]

While in the Reunion Islands, the Indian Community does not face any persecution as such. But since the heydays of colonialism, there has been a push to assimilate Indians in

142 *Diaspora and Nation-Building*

the ways of the French. The belief in the superiority of things French held by many, probably most, Frenchmen working in the colonial administrations meant that they would tend to promote French things. Thus, the Indian immigrants in Reunion Island were completely assimilated in the French system through various political, educational and cultural institutions. The persons of Indian origin (PIOs) in Reunion no longer speak their mother tongue apart from a few phrases. They use Creole in their daily conversation, be it in the family or in commercial transactions.

Having undergone a process of veritable de-culturalisation through the assimilation process from the 1946-1980s has left the Indian community in Reunion Island in search for its roots. This systematic erosion of identity has in some ways devalued the political, economic and human rights of the Indian community, even though they constitute a little over 31 percent of the 8,02,000 strong population of the island, a sizeable number.

Another stark example is that of the Indian community in Sri Lanka facing persecution at the hands of the Sinhalese, which has, in turn, led to a state system which denies them the political power, employment, educational opportunities and basic human rights which a citizen of every country is worthy of. After decades of being systematically marginalised in Sri Lanka since independence from the British, Black July in 1983 saw the slaughter of an unknown number of Tamils. Estimates range between 400 and 3,000 Tamils killed and perhaps 25,000 injured. This was the onset of large-scale civil war. Continuing for decades in fits and starts, the armed conflict ended with a massive military operation by the Sri Lankan government forces against Tamils struggling for an independent state. In an unfortunate chapter of the war's closing days, in May of 2009, the White Flag Incident saw the killing of Tamils who thought they had arranged for surrender. The 'resolution' of the conflict has left the diaspora increased by refugees, perhaps 90,000

Indian Diaspora: Contribution of... 143

Tamil war widows, and has attracted the attention of the world concerned about the ongoing strife faced by Tamils in Sri Lanka. The treatment of the Indian community in Sri Lanka has brought to the forefront glaring human rights abuses for which relief efforts have not been as steadfast as the present situation demands.

From the above examples, we can see that identity is one of several fundamental human needs that underlie many conflicts. It is the primary issue in most conflicts. This does not mean that different identities cannot co-exist. If adaptability and co-existence are fundamental to nature, the same can hold true for humans as well, provided a conscience effort is made on behalf of all and especially those in power to give to others space to exist, equality of opportunity to realise their hopes and aspirations and ensure basic human rights to themselves and to others.

Today human rights are of great importance. Under various international conventions, governments are not allowed to violate the rights of minorities, such as their right in enjoying non-discriminatory policies in order to take measures to support minorities to maintain their identity. International institutions like the United Nations and international human rights charters like the International Treaty of civil and political rights should actively take part and be enforced in ensuring the basic human rights of the Indian diaspora.

From Challenges to Participation: An Opportunity

The main problem faced by the Indian diaspora is participation in the economic, social, political and democratic institutions in their respective adopted countries. This challenge is unique as it is not a challenge, but an opportunity for the nations to let the vibrant Indian community showcase their talents and to provide them the opportunity so they can help in the process of nation-building. In many countries like Madagascar, Fiji, Malaysia, Sri Lanka, Reunion Islands, etc., the

144 *Diaspora and Nation-Building*

Indian diaspora is facing proscription from the mainstream or apprehension from the indigenous population or the numerically superior ethnicities.

In Madagascar, the Indian community, though economically strong, faces adverse government policies as the indigenous Malagasies consider the economic empowerment of the Indians as a challenge to their own economic interests. Hence, the socio-political status of Indians in Madagascar is quite low because Indians have always been viewed with suspicion by not only those who were in power, but also by Malagasy people. Although living for many generations, many people of Indian origin have been denied Malagasy citizenship. They need residence permits. They are considered as foreigners and laws of foreigners regulate their community activities, prohibiting certain professions to them and the acquisition of immovable without prior approval of the public authorities. Lack of citizenship property restricts their active engagement in political activities of Madagascar. Social and cultural exclusiveness practised by persons of Indian origin and their high economic status has made them a hated community. They are seen as exploiters and are victim to any political and civil unrest in the country.[3]

While in Fiji, the situation is not comforting either. The Indians, who were primarily engaged in agriculture, have been denied basic land ownership rights as Fiji remained in the hands of the Fijians, making land-ownership of Indians in Fiji next to impossible. Fiji became independent in 1970, but a series of military coups (starting in 1987) and the resulting political instability as well as continuing racial tensions led to an exodus of Indians from Fiji. Lal sums up the problematic situation of Indians in Fiji as follows:

"After more than a century, Indo-Fijians still struggle for political equality in the land of their birth. The deeply felt but often unacknowledged need of the human soul to belong, to

Indian Diaspora: Contribution of... 145

have a place of one's own, to be rooted, is denied to them. How long, they ask, should people live in a place before they are allowed to call it home? 'From Immigration to Emigration'; that may in time come to be the epitaph of Fiji's Indo-Fijian community."[5]

As discussed earlier, in Malaysia, Indians continue to be looked down upon. It is difficult for Indians to obtain a fair chance of development as they're considered to be outsiders. The following statistics collected by various sources indicate the marginalisation and deprivation of the Indians in Malaysia in every aspect of life:

- Seventy percent of the two million Indians are very poor or poor; the national average poverty level is a mere 2.8 percent (Ponnusamy 2009: 27).
- Less than 1 percent of Malaysia's education budget goes to Indian schools, even though Indians comprise about 8 percent of the total population (South Asian Voice 2008).
- Indians' participation in the civil services declined from about 40 percent in 1957 to about 2 percent in 2007 (Kuppuswamy 2010).
- About 90 percent of the armed forces personnel are from the majority Malay Muslims (Ramakrishnan 2011).
- 78 percent of the government services are occupied by Malays, while Indians share only 4 percent (Ramakrishnan 2011).
- Indians comprise 60 percent of the urban squatters and 41 percent of all beggars (The Economist, February 22, 2003).
- 95 percent of Malaysian victims shot dead by the police and 90 percent of the deaths in police and prison custody victims are Indians (Ponnusamy 2009: 32).

146   *Diaspora and Nation-Building*

The above mentioned instances tell us that there is a severe problem of exclusion faced by the Indian diaspora. To turn this challenge into an opportunity there needs to be a multifaceted effort, wherein participation of the Indian diaspora in the local affairs and institutions of their adopted countries needs to be encouraged. For example, create a consensus among the indigenous population through concerted efforts by the political and social leaders that the outsiders are a part of their community and that their development is symbiotic to the development of their nation and themselves. A shining example in this regard is Seychelles where the Indian community has done well in education and other sectors of the economy and particularly in self-employment. The Indian community has a substantial presence and diverse spread in this beautiful island country. Many of them are occupying important positions in Seychelles contributing substantially to the development and prosperity of this country. They are bringing technological advancement in the country and, most importantly, they are one of the biggest employers of local population. Indians in Seychelles enjoy an equal political status vis-a-vis other communities. It is a matter of great pride that the Indians here are respected and loved by the local people and there has been a great degree of cross cultural fertilisation over the two hundred odd years since the first Indians reached these islands.

Such shining examples give us an idea of the contribution Indian diaspora can make in their adopted countries, if provided with the right opportunities and equality in all spheres of society. The progress of the Indian diaspora is directly proportional to the progress of their nations and that of their institutions that is socio-economic, political and, above all, democratic. Hence, there is a pressing need to avail these opportunities to the Indian community in order to make them a part of the mainstream.

Conclusion

Indian diaspora, although varied and widespread, carried with them socio-cultural baggage which consisted, among other things, a predefined social identity, a set of religious beliefs, a framework of norms and values governing family and kinship organisation, food habits and language. The migration did not cut them away from the vivid memory of living in India and in many ways, retained physical and emotional contact with their homeland. This phenomenon was accelerated due to the hardships of living in an alien culture and community totally removed from the background they hail from. This facet of migration makes them distinct.

Though, over the years, this connect with their roots has been forgotten to an extent, but they still remain as Indian as ever. Our brothers and sisters have faced and are still facing huge challenges. But I'm sure, the values of democratic tradition of the Indian civilisation and culture as encapsulated in the Vedas will help them overcome these challenges, which declare unequivocally: AJYESTHAASO AKANISTHAASA YETE SAM BHRAATARO VAAVRUDHUH SOUBHAGAYA—'No one is superior or inferior; all are brothers; all should strive for the interest of all and progress collectively'.

In such a time when the world community is getting divided into different groups and ideologies, the Indian diaspora can be a shining light and be the teachers of tolerance, equality, brotherhood and all the other ideals which represent our great culture. These ideals need to be put into action, to safeguard the present and the future of our brothers and sisters in their adopted nations.

Notes and References

1. http://www.refworld.org/pdfid/525fbfda4.pdf
2. http://www.e-ir.info/2013/02/06/challenges-to-the-rights-of-malaysians-of-indian-descent/

148 *Diaspora and Nation-Building*

3. http://shodhganga.inflibnet.ac.in/bitstream/10603/16671/7/07_chapter%202.pdf
4. http://www.zora.uzh.ch/id/eprint/100259/1/HundtHomeDiaspora.pdf.
5. (Brij.V.Lal, 2004)
6. http://www.e-ir.info/2013/02/06/challenges-to-the-rights-of-malaysians-of-indian-descent/.

□

Role of Indian Diaspora in Nation-Building: The Mauritian Experience

—Dr. Sarita Boodhoo

Introduction

Indian presence on Mauritian soil has given a new political definition to the whole concept of nation-building. Since the arrival of Indians in various phases of our history but particularly with the *Girmitiya* Indian Indentured labour system as from 2nd November 1834, a new socio-political-economic script developed on the island, that would see the island transforming its narrative over a period of two centuries from a colonial rule to an independent nation largely dominated by a majority democratic rule. The nation-builders since independence have taken the initiative to develop nationhood through well-geared government programmes guaranteeing free education, free Health Services for all, affordable low-cost housing and a Welfare State with modern infrastructural support. Achievement of a remarkable degree of stable political environment, social harmony and cohesion and economic growth that would make Mauritius an enviable global financial hub embracing Fin-tech systems with E-Government. Bracing itself to manage a Blue Economy in the future with its huge Exclusive Economic Zone (EEZ) over the vast Indian Ocean, it is now becoming a massive Ocean State.

150 *Diaspora and Nation-Building*

With a population of nearly 1.3 million, Mauritius is the success story of a harmonious plural society with several ethnic groups, multi-religious, multi-linguistic and cultural traditions counterfeiting a prosperous multi-faceted society moving from original Lower Income Economy to Middle-Upper Middle Income Economy towards High Income Economy Status by 2020.

The phenomenal demography rise of the Indian population as from 1860 that would keep a balance of 2/3 of the total population till date would mark a watershed in the future political life and destiny of the island-nation and its future course of socio-economic development. Mauritius is a vivid example of the immense contribution of Indians towards the development of a host country. However, till date, 70% of the land is owned by descendants of white oligarchy.

Nevertheless this tiny island of 790 sq miles or 2,040 sq kms area in the Indian Ocean has no minerals, unless we tap the jackpot with petroleum in our EEZ. It has depended entirely on the strength of its remarkable human resources. The Indian immigrants and their descendants, a majority population in the country, have learnt to co-exist with other immigrants and dominant colonial forces. Mauritius was until four centuries ago a totally uninhabited island. By sheer force of their majority, hard work and sacrifice and a civilisational ethos and inherent wisdom based on peace, sharing and justice, they brought along with them from ancient India, they managed to rise from squalor to government.

The Indian diaspora has contributed immensely in the making of Mauritius right from the Dutch and French periods.

The plantation economy of the 19th century demanded a workforce in various colonies, whether British, French, Dutch and others. This entailed a huge mobilisation of indentured labour from India, the jewel of British Empire, amongst others. Over 90 years of the indenture system, some two million Indians moved from India to various countries, namely

Mauritius, South Africa, Fiji, Singapore, Malaysia, Surinam, Guyana, Trinidad and Tobago, Guadeloupe, Martinique, Reunion Island, etc. Mauritius, however, received the greatest number of *girmitiyas*.

French Period

Mauritius was the '*first post*' of the British of this lucrative transaction of human labour – '*great experience*' as it was called. But the advent of Indian immigration to Mauritius was a much earlier process with the periodical movement of Indian soldiers, seafarers, '*sepoys*', political prisoners, free artisans and engineers in the 18th century. The Indian presence in Mauritius can be traced as far back as the Dutch period in the 17th century (1638-1710) when they introduced sugarcane from Batavia as well as some menial workers from Bengal.

During the French period, as early as 1726, came free artisans, engineers and traders from the French '*comptoirs*' – trading posts of Pondicherry, Karaikkal, Mahé, Yanaon and Chandanagore in Bengal. But also from Tranquebar, Coromandel from the Malabar Coast. The place names of Tranquebar and Coromandel on the outskirts of the Capital Port-Louis and the use of the term '*Malabar*' albeit in a pejorative way testify to this determining Indian presence during the French period. They came as early as 1721.

The soldiers, who came during the early British period when the British took over the island from the French in 1810 were known as '*Sepoys*' or in Creole '*Sipaye*' from the Indian word '*Sipahi*'. These early Indians in Mauritius were skilled workers and master craftsmen. They built roads, storehouses, administrative buildings, canals and aqueducts to carry drinking water. The cobbled streets of Port Louis bear their prints.

Mahé de Labourdonnais, the erstwhile French Governor of '*Ile Maurice*' and *Isle de Bourbon (Reunion Island)*, known then as '*Les Mascaregnes*', was dispatched from French '*Comptoirs*'

152   *Diaspora and Nation-Building*

in South India in 1735 to administer Mauritius. He displayed outstanding bravery, and in five years of administration, his vision, skills, organisational abilities and entrepreneurship, he created the port, the harbour and laid down much of early Port Louis. This with a massive influx of free Indian craftsmen as importing labour from Europe was costly. Some of the buildings constructed then can still be visible, facing the waterfront harbour.

The remarkable impressive wooden building of the Legislative Assembly (Parliament House) is a rare piece of architecture built by craftsmen and builders from India during Mahé de Labourdonnais's time. They built various other infrastructural support and worked as market gardeners too. They were also skilled carpenters and masons. They served as dock workers too. They were jewellers, shoe makers and tailors. They also formed part of the French naval and military force. They built coastal forts and roads. They were so enterprising that they became contractors and builders and officers in the French administration. Quite a few became absorbed as members of the 'coloured' creole élite. Some received generous land grants from French planters. They themselves became employers of slaves and even owned one or two sugar factories of the time.

Resourceful traders from Madras came to Mauritius and settled in Port Louis during this period. They set up a thriving trade and commerce in Port Louis. This led to a well-structured commercial venture still largely under the grip of the dominant class of Franco-Mauritians. They were also versatile shipping agents and carried on the lucrative business of importing goods from India.

Also came some Parsi merchants, and *'Mehmons'* from Cutch and Surat in Gujarat in who settled and carried business in Port-Louis. Much of these early Indians except for the Guajarati community came to be merged in the creole population through conversion and inter-marriage which is

Role of Indian Diaspora in Nation-Building...   153

reflected in their Indian surnames till date. Some street names in Port, Louis such as *Tanjore, Goa, Velore* and *Calicut,* testify to their presence in the capital city. Moreover, this is how two important segments of Port Louis were known as *Camp des Lascars* (today's Plaine Verte area) mostly Muslim mariners and sailors, and *Camp des Malabars,* mostly South Indian origin.

Unfortunately, this part of Indian contribution in the making of Mauritius has not been highlighted enough.

The Girmitiya Period

The need for labour force to work in the sugar plantations after the abolition of slavery led to the indentureship of Indian labour. The British masters and the French oligarchy were desperate and were facing ruins. There already existed a lucrative trade of labour from the Presidency of *Bihar, Awadh, Bengal* and *Orissa* towards the newly created tea gardens of Darjeeling in Assam. The plough for such contract labour for the colonies led a gold mine discovery. The first batch of *girmitiyas* (*apbhrmnsa* form of English word 'Agreement') – on contract labour of five years arriving on 2nd November 1834 on the Atlas even before the date of official proclamation of abolition of slavery in British Parliament on 1st February 1935 proved how anxious were the French planters and British administrators in quest of new labour. Thus began a system which ended officially on 17 April 1918, but continued till 31 May 1924 after the decisive report of Kunwar Maharaj Singh despatched by the British Raj to look into the dreary/dismal conditions of living of the *girmitiyas,* injustice and oppression and suppression suffered.

The new labour system on contract of five years led to more than 450,000 *girmitiyas* arrival and settlement in Mauritius. Some went back upon termination of their contract, but others made '*a home away from home*' in Mauritius.

The *girmitiyas* not only helped to build the local sugar

154 *Diaspora and Nation-Building*

economy as a strong firm springboard for future economic development and prosperity of Mauritius, but contributed in producing the wealth of the oligarchy plantocrats as well as the world economy based on the high price that sugar fetched as a prized commodity in manufacturing various new industries such as chocolate, etc.

The plight of the *girmitiyas* was not an easy one. Several Commissions of enquiries had to be instituted for the betterment of their lot. It was a sheer exploitation of man by man, not much different from the earlier system of slavery.

With their sweat, tears and blood, they nurtured and raised the lush green sugarcane plantations that had formed the backbone of the Mauritian economy. Their souls, muscles, sinews joined in one great propelling force to resist humiliation, exploitation, injustice and insolent might and abject poverty. After their 5 years' contract, they bought little pieces of land and set up their villages based on the home model they had left behind. They built *baithkas* not only to teach their children moral and social values of Ramayana, but also as a meeting place for social redress and discuss the price of sugar.

They were able to resist because they carried in their veins the wisdom and civilisational ethos of ancient India which they brought with them through *Ramayana, Mahabharata,* and *Hanuman Chalisa.* These irrigated their mind with the principles of faith, sustenance, and tenacity to bear, love, tolerance, forgiveness and patience. They mustered all their energies to survive not only physically, but morally and intellectually. They faced insolent might without bending their knees. Quite a few *girmitiyas* like the *Gujadhurs,* the *Ramdins,* the *Gaureesungkurs,* the *Dookhee Gangahs,* the *Seegobind* families rose very quickly to become prominent small planters. The *Currimjee Jeewanjee, Chettiar, Tulsidas, Ghanty, Bahemia* and other erstwhile traders who followed the *girmitiyas* to set up their trade in providing the *dal, roti, rice* and *clothings,* are examples of successful businessmen and traders. The *sonar*

Role of Indian Diaspora in Nation-Building... 155

community also thrived as the *girmitiyas* invested largely in gold and silver jewellery for their wives.

In fact, as early as 1860, after the whites parcelled out waste lands known as the *'Grand Morcellement'*, many of the Indians who bought land, who would be the greatest land owners after the whites and their properties could range from 5 acres to several hundred acres.

The trade and commerce of this community is typified by the Mauritian currency note. First of all, the British retained the rupee currency note and paise, aathanne, char anne (introduced in India by Sher Shah Suri in the 16th century) as prevalent in India to facilitate fiduciary transactions. Moreover, besides English, the notes are inscribed in two Indian languages, namely Tamil and Hindi, including Gujarati for the numeral denominations. This is maintained till date.

Gandhiji's Arrival

The arrival of Mohandas Karamchand Gandhi, not yet Mahatma, intrepid lawyer from South Africa on a chance, halt when his ship bound for India berthed in Port Louis for revitalisation and repairs, in October 1901, brought a turning point in the crystallisation of the *Girmitiyas* consciousness in shaping their future and rise like the phoenix from the ashes. At the reception, given by the wealthy Gujarati Muslim and Tamil merchants and traders in Taher Bagh, Port Louis, Gandhi exhorted them to join politics.

To the masses, he visited in Rivière du Rempart and other places, he told them to educate their children and send them to school. The fear of conversion and need for help on the newly established small family plots of sedentary farming, of rearing cows, goats, etc., led them to keep their children at home.

Gandhiji himself could not spend more time in Mauritius than some 19 days. But he sent valiant Manilal Doctor, a young Guajarati French knowing fearless barrister who, since his arrival on the island set to redress the fate of the oppressed

156   *Diaspora and Nation-Building*

Indian planters and labourers and take up their cudgels, in Court matters.

Manilal Doctor would help them raise their voice and fight injustice through the setting up of the *'Hindustani'*, a trilingual Guajarati-English and Hindi newspaper. He helped them in setting up the Mauritius Co-operative Bank to finance their small plantations and businesses as they were denied loans from the Mauritius Commercial Bank owned by white planters and built largely by slave compensation money.

Manilal Doctor also encouraged a band of volunteers in the setting up of the Arya Samaj movement in 1911. This would help mobilise Indian masses and create awareness for social mobility and education. Thousands of Indians gained social recognition and dignity through the transmission of Vedic Knowledge and opening of Hindi schools and *Kanya Vidyalayas*. Hundreds of *pracharaks* and *pracharikas* were trained in Hindi to teach *Satyarth Prakash* of Swami Dayanand Saraswati to the Indian masses. The Arya Samaj movement gave a voice to the destitutes and also kept the community united. The main seat of Arya Sabha was set up at the Champ de Mars in Port Louis became the steering hub of the whole machinery of regular mobilisation.

In the following decades, voices of young Indian elites rose on the firmament. The contribution of individual Indo-Mauritian intellectuals and professionals, such as R.K. Boodhun, Rajsumer Lallah, Dr. Idris Goomany, Dr. A. Gaffoor Jeetoo, D.M.D. Atchia in articulating their bold thoughts and opinions at national level against injustice is worthy. Some Hindi newspapers came up like the *Arya Vir, Aryodaye, Mauritius Indian Times*, etc.

In 1935, a small group of Indian intellectuals met to celebrate the centenary of Indian Indentured arrival. They brought out a Journal for the Commemoration, along with others, Dr. Kissoon Singh Hazareesingh, later the first Director of the Mahatma Gandhi Institute in 1975, Dr. Seewoosagur

Role of Indian Diaspora in Nation-Building... 157

Ramgoolam just back from his ten-year medical studies in the United Kingdom, R.K. Boodhun and others were active members of the committee. Aunath Beejadhur, later Minister of Education, wrote his book '*Les Indiens à l'île Maurice*' in 1935. This celebration of 100 years of *Girmitiyas* in Mauritius was a turning point in the greater sensitisation of the Indians towards socio-political awakening. Several Arya Samaj stalwarts rose on the horizon like Pandit Cashinath Kistoe, Pandit Gayasingh and Guruprasad Duljeetlal, Mohunlal Mohit.

Trade Union movements for the exploited sugar labourers and artisans were established in the 1940s by Pandit Ramnarain, Pandit Jugdambi, Chander Bhageerutty and others. They would join forces with the Creole artisans and dockers to demand further redress and amelioration of working conditions.

During one such prayer meeting in a *baithka* in Belle Vue Harel, a young Indian woman with child Anjalay Devi Coopen was gunned down (27 September 1943) by the police. She is the epitome of martyrdom in the cause of Indian labourers and celebrated annually as a national heroine.

Pandit Basdeo Bissoondayal came back from Tertiary studies in Lahore and at the Calcutta University where he obtained his M.A. in English in 1939. Largely influenced by Gandhiji's movement and the Arya Samaj movement in Lahore, an Arya Samaj hub, he imbibed the teachings of the Vedas and Upanishads. He gave hundreds of fiery sermons and cemented the matrix of the Indo-Mauritian masses further. He brought to end the ignominious '*Lecourse Malbar*', a derogatory horse race at the Champ de Mars for the Indians for which the white plantocrats released the labourers to attend. He revived several Hindu festivals, such as *Ganga Asnan, Holi and Maha Shivratri*. He encouraged the enactment of small village plays such as *Ram Lilas*.

At the same time Dr. Seewoosagur Ramgoolam's return from UK in 1935 freshly imbibed with Indian Independence

158   *Diaspora and Nation-Building*

movement strategies juxtaposed as he was with students of the London wing of Indian National Congress, such as Krishna Menon was a determining factor in the political awakening of the Indians in Mauritius. In UK, he not only earned his medical degree, but he also had a rare intellectual ear for English Literature and Indian Philosophy. He rubbed shoulders with Yeats and the Fabian socialists. He also would proofread the biography of Subhash Chandra Bose. With the Indian National Congress Youth Wing, he was embattled with the fire of Indian Independence.

Upon his return, he would go to distant villages all over the island and galvanise the exploited toiling labouring people through his *'mass movement'* (in his own words). He went from *Baithka* to *Baithka* and addressed the people in Bhojpuri and aroused them to their economic, political and social rights. He would soon be elected as the leader of the newly created Labour Party. Pandit Sahadeo – another Indo-Mauritian stalwart, joined forces with the creole leaders, such as Guy Rozemont, Maurice Curé to organise the first-ever 1st May Day meeting at Champ de Mars in 1938 which would definitely be a stepping stone towards the redress for working classes.

Literacy Test

In 1948, the British Government brought about a new Constitution for Mauritius. Property qualifications for the franchise were abolished. However, the people had to go through a simple *literacy test.* The literacy test was held in the move for greater democratic representation and *adult suffrage* for all Mauritians. Pandit Basdeo Bissoondayal mobilised thousands to teach them to sign their names in Hindi, Tamil, Telugu, Marathi, Urdu and other Indian languages. This would bring a revolution in the franchise. So far, only the landed property owners, namely the wealthy white plantocrats could be elected to the government machinery and formulate laws and policies. The literacy test would open wide the sluice gates of political democracy to the Indo-Mauritians for the first time in the political history of Mauritius. For the first time out of nineteen elected Members, eleven Indo-Mauritians were elected and entered the Legislative Assembly as representatives of the rural Indian people.

Such stalwarts as Renganaden Seeneevassen, Sir Veerasawmy Ringadoo, Aunath Beejadhur (who would be the 2nd Minister of Education after Sir Seewoosagur Ramgoolam), Bikramsing Ramlallah, Sookdeo Bissoondayal, Sir Harilal Ranchoddas Vaghjee, Satcam Boolell, Dr. Seewoosagur Ramgoolam, Anerood Jugnauth are prominent sons of the *girmitiyas* (except for Sir Harilal Vaghjee – eminent Speaker of the Legislative Assembly, Gujarati-speaking) who spearheaded the upward movements for the downtrodden.

Political awakening, demands for social and educational amelioration, were among the main objectives of the political leaders. The move for Independence of Mauritius gathered steam. This move was a growing menace to the white oligarchy and their plantation and financial interests. There were dastardly attacks in a section of the Mauritian press controlled by them. Such statements as Indo-Mauritians are not Mauritians and they should go back to India were often aired. The fear of a Hindu hegemony was looming large and the fear of attachment of Mauritius after Independence to India was felt as a menace to the white planters. Dr. Seewoosagur Ramgoolam with his Fabian socialist leaning was viewed as a *'communist'*. One would recall here how the British under Sir Winston Churchill did everything to topple Dr. Cheddi Jagan of Guyana, because of his communist leanings.

As the press attacks on the Indians became more intense, virulent and vitriolic, Indian intellectuals and professionals and thinking people got together to decide a future move of actions. The Nalanda Bookshop at 28 Bourbon Street, Port Louis was the meeting hub. The need for a newspaper to

160 *Diaspora and Nation-Building*

retaliate and press for Independence was urgently felt. There was already the '*Advance*' daily appearing in French set up by Seewoosagur Ramgoolam and others which was formerly edited by Aunauth Beejadhur and later Geerjaparsad Ramloll. Sookdeo Bissoondoyal had established the *Zamana* newspaper. Bikramsing Ramlallah, would give up his government job as a teacher to fund and edit the Mauritius Times, an opinion paper in English, to mobilise for Independence, amd retaliate the press attacks of the oligarchy.

After several constitutional talks held at Lancaster House in England, finally, Dr. Seewoosagur Ramgoolam of the Labour Party joined forces with rival Indo-Mauritian Leaders, such as Abdool Razack Mohammed, Founder and Leader of '*Comité d'Action Musulman*' (Muslim Action Committee Party) and Sookdeo Bissoondoyal, Leader and Founder of IFB (Independent Forward Block) inspired by Subhash Chandra Bose's Party, to move as one bloc for Independence. At that time, Sir Anerood Jugnauth was a Legislative Member with Sookdeo Bissoondoyal. Earlier, to move for Equal Opportunity in the Civil Service for Hindus who were ostracised from Government jobs not to speak of Private Sector which was sealed to them like a clam, Anerood Jugnauth had set up the Mauritius Hindu Congress. General Elections were held on 7 August 1967.

Eventually, the Indian community in Mauritius forgot and set aside their petty ideological differences, personal interests and ambitions. They founded the Independence Party which was victorious in gaining Independence on 12 March 1968. This is a landmark step in nation-building through the visionary decision and farsightedness of the Indo-Mauritian political leaders. Sir Seewoosagur Ramgoolam had retained the 12 March, a symbolical date – as Gandhiji's Dandi Salt March that would set the sun on the British Empire.

In their perceptiveness and judicious policy decisions, the Mauritian Indian leaders were able to establish the ground for a long-term and lasting political and social stability in a

Role of Indian Diaspora in Nation-Building... 161

plural society. The Indian system of *Panchayat* as legacied by the *girmitiyas*, set up under a *banyan tree* and in *baithkas* was, thus, incorporated in a political system of democracy based on the Westminster model which led to the creation of a successful Welfare State.

Another aspect of the farsightedness of the Founding Father of the Nation is that immediately after the 1968 Independence, Sir Seewoosagur Ramgoolam, the first and new Prime Minister forged a coalition with rival Sir Gaëtan Duval of Opposition and Leader of the PMSD (*Parti Mauricien Social Démocrate*). It would be recalled that the 1967 General Elections brought a cleavage along ethnic divisions. The sugar barons had largely supported the PMSD. 44% of the population voted against Independence largely composed of urban creole votes. Thousands of coloured and creole bureaucrats and officers who had manned all the top level government establishments, left their good jobs and salaries, sold their majestic villas and houses for peanuts and went to settle in Australia, France and South Africa in fear of a Hindu hegemony due to the aggressive anti-Indian political campaign.

As a result, there was a vacuum in the Establishment. At the same time, thousands of Indian youths were deprived of elementary and secondary education for decades due to poverty. There were only three State Secondary Schools – Royal College Curepipe (Boys) (Founded: 1791), Royal College Port Louis (Boys) (Founded: 1799) and Queen Elizabeth College (Girls) that also built in 1950. Other secondary schools were aided Convent Schools which were fee paying where Indian students were largely marginalised and which the poor could not afford. With the Independence and Indian government's generous support, the doors of India were open. Poor students could hardly afford to go to Europe and South Africa for higher education.

After Independence and with the sugar boom in 1975, thousands of poor students from rural areas went for

162 *Diaspora and Nation-Building*

graduation to Indian universities. At one time, Chandigarh was even known as Mauritius Garh! With their degrees in hand, they filled the posts left vacant by the frightened urban creoles and coloureds.

The Stable Civil Service or Government Functionary set up by the British was taken over by the new recruits armed with their degrees and Indian diplomas. Many went to study medicine also either in India or Russia and Eastern European countries. The effective and efficient bureaucrats in policy-making and implantation of actions of the Government have kept the government machinery well-oiled and smooth-running.

Sir Seewoosagur Ramgoolam created besides the Welfare State, several schemes that would provide jobs and develop the new nascent nation, such as the Economic Processing Zone (EPZ) set up several new State Secondary Schools all over the island, opened the University of Mauritius, encouraged new disciplines, in the University Faculties, constructed new Modern High-ways, linking airport to the whole of the country, set up new manufacturing factories and built new hospitals.

His sagacious foreign policy of opting to join the newly formed Organisation of African Unity (OAU), now African Union and offering to host the first International Conference of OAU in Mauritius (2–6 July 1976) was a breakthrough in our international diplomacy that would set Mauritius on the world map and as one of the newly emerging African countries. We would also be part of the Regional groups, such as SADC, COMESSA and, later, member of the Indian Ocean Rim Association (IORA) whose Secretariat is in Mauritius.

The Indian Government since the very beginning was the most benign companion/partner to accompany and assist Mauritius in its new emerging role as a young nation. The relationship between India and Mauritius is a privileged, special and unique one, forged by blood, history and civilisational ethos. As soon as India became independent, Mauritius was the first post where the Indian High Commissioner would be appointed in the name of Shri Dharma Yash Dev. The Indian Mission in Mauritius delighted the village masses by sending its 'Mobile Cinema Van' to show and acquaint us with Indian music, culture and documentaries showing its development, even prior to the appointment of the first Indian High Commissioner.

The multitude of Indian aids in terms of scholarships, capacity-building, infrastructure and, to date, the Metro Express, State-of-the-Art Scheme, the Coast Guard, security of the sea has guided and groomed Mauritius in moving from a Low-Income Monocrop Economy to a Middle-Income Economy expected to rise to a High-Income Economy by 2020.

The many Institutions like the Mahatma Gandhi and Rabindranath Tagore Institutes, the Jawaharlal Nehru Hospital, the Rajiv Gandhi Science Centre, the Indira Gandhi Centre for Indian Culture, the World Hindi Secretariat, the Shri Atal Bihari Vajpayee Cyber Tower/Cyber City, the New Supreme Court, the Students Free Tablets, the Swami Vivekananda International Convention Centre are so many aspects of Capacity-Building which have helped Mauritius in its affirmation of a new prosperous nation.

The Republic State

The next step in the process of the creation of a Nation was the accession of Mauritius to the Status of a Republic under the leadership of Sir Anerood Jugnauth. His economic miracle as from 1983 would largely take the country to its present success story of an emerging small Island State transformed to an Ocean State.

The principles of peace, justice and liberty as enshrined in the Mauritian anthem *'Glory to thee Motherland'* are key symbolical words that have seen a peaceful transformation and harmonious co-existence amidst a multi-ethnic, multi-religious and multi-lingual society which has accelerated the nation-building process.

164 *Diaspora and Nation-Building*

The celebration this year of 50 years of Independence 2018 in a grant national fervour and manifestation by the Government of Mauritius has served to bring to one and all the essence of the Spirit of '*Lame Dan Lame*' – '*Hand in Hand*' – '*Hanthon mein Hanth*' in the process of the consolidation of the nation.

Today, young Pravind Jugnauth, Prime Minister as the symbol of a young nation reflects a stable, poised and balanced moderate leadership. His blueprint for Mauritius 2030 is a transformational paradigm – Way Forward which was reflected in the Budget Speech of 14 June 2018.

The adamantine and bold policy of modernising the country's infrastructure through the Metro Express with the unflinching support of Shri Narendra Modi ji is the contribution of a judicious policy of bringing together the public and private sectors to work in a Win-Win strategy.

The emergence of a tiny monocrop sugar-based Economy from the *Girmitiya* period where the Indian was merely a passive watcher of the development of the country, though his sinews and muscles had serviced this same development to a Smart Economy where he now leads the Government, activates and generates the development process of the Nation, reflects the rapid transformation of Mauritian society over two centuries with the Indian diaspora as a key player in Nation-Building.

□

The Contribution of Women Towards Nation-Building in Mauritius: A Qualitative Study

—Beebeejaun-Muslum Zareen

Mauritius, an island situated in the Indian Ocean with a population of around 1.2 million (Stats Mauritius, 2017) is made up of five different ethnic groups, namely Indians, Creoles, Muslims, Chinese and Europeans. Muslims and Hindus came to Mauritius as Indentured Immigrants during the 1800s and the early 1900s and are also known as People of Indian Origin (PIO). The latter came mainly between 1829 and 1910. It is estimated that between 100,000 and 105,000 female Indian and non-Indian immigrants came to the Mauritian shores to work as Indentured labourers. They were mostly between the ages of 10 and 50. Over the years, the PIOs have worked really hard and moved Mauritius up to a middle-income country.

Often cited as a success story, Mauritius has successfully transformed itself from a monocrop economy to a high upper-middle-income country over the last 50 years. Today, Mauritius is among the most successful economies in Africa. Currently, Mauritius tops sub-Saharan economies and ranks 45th globally. According to the Global Competitiveness Report 2016-2017 released by the World Economic Forum, it ranks

166 *Diaspora and Nation-Building*

1st in Africa and 49th worldwide in the Doing Business 2017 report, released by the World Bank Group.

For a small island economy like Mauritius deprived of natural resources, having to adjust to a falling birth rate and an ageing population whilst also envisaging to become a high-income economy, harnessing its talent and human capital becomes essential. Fully capitalising on the female labour force has tremendous potential to spur growth, enable the attainment of higher-income status and address the challenges of population ageing. Nevertheless, economic growth is not the only the reason why female participation in the labour force matters. Higher workforce participation can reduce the fiscal pressures associated with welfare support, serve inclusion and equity goals and enable women to unlock their capabilities and "expand their freedoms to live long, healthy and creative lives" (UNDP, 2010).

Appropriate use of women's talent and skills not only provides families with more economic independence, but also increases women's self-confidence and social respectability (World Bank, 2009). Moreover, higher levels of female employment allow government investments in education to be used more efficiently as women use their acquired talents productively in the economy of the country. Mauritius was the country which was mentioned as 'doomed' by experts like Professor Mead and Titmuss, mainly due to over-population and its reliance over a monocrop economy. However, the citizens, including the PIO (both males and females) have proved them wrong through their labour and perseverance. PIO women toiled hard in agricultural lands and gradually they have emerged to become nation-builders by participating actively in the economy (Moser, 1999).

The role of women in economic development has attracted much interest in academia and international organisations, such as the International Monetary Fund (IMF) and the United Nations (UN). They have argued for the importance of

The Contribution of Women Towards Nation-Building... 167

female emancipation for successful economic development. One of the most cited ground-breaking studies in this field is from Ester Boserup (1971). Boserup focusses on women's role, particularly in the early stages of development and industrialisation. She finds that women's position in society, their levels of education, and their roles in the family may act as important triggers of economic development. Gender equality is likely to be beneficial for economic growth as it tends to be accompanied by increased levels of education and decreased mortality rates (Kabeer et al., 2013). There are scholars who have focussed on the potential macroeconomic gains of increasing gender equality and the inclusion of women.

Additionally, the IMF (2013) points out that increasing female labour force participation may be an effective aid for economic growth for countries struggling with ageing populations. Inclusion of women can support economic growth when the workforce becomes increasingly small due to the increasing withdrawal of previously active people into retirement. The inclusion of women in wider spheres of professional work could be beneficial from a business perspective as well. Women could provide a wider range of opinions that could be more fitting to markets oriented towards a female consumer basis (CED, 2012; CAHRS, 2011).

Nation-building is a long, time-consuming process of constructing and fashioning a national identity. Economic, social, and political development, and institutions which protect human rights and provide for the rule of law, are important not only to post-conflict-peace-building, but to nation-building at any stage of development or any stage of conflict also. At the same time, it forges a sense of unity, a sense of belonging and this leads the way towards success. National development is the ability of a county or countries to improve the social welfare of its people, by providing social amenities like quality education, potable water, transportation, infrastructure, medical care, and so on. When people feel

168 *Diaspora and Nation-Building*

'in', they voluntarily contribute to all facets of a country's development.

In this way, the traditional role of women from history has always been child bearing/rearing and housekeeping which would often include subsistence agricultural activities. In those days, the Mauritian family was merely a unit of production when one would work as a team in agricultural lands. The economic activity was centred on the family members. At the same time, the Indentured Immigrants in Mauritius had already learnt the value of education and would send both boys and girls to attend at least primary education without distinction and till today, gender parity is achieved through equal access to education for both boys and girls.

However, given the nature of its patriarchal society, it is understood that Mauritian women should take care of their families while shouldering other responsibilities at work (Suntoo, 2003). Mauritian women worked in the Export Processing Zone (EPZ) as passive, docile and hard workers who rarely complained about the poor working conditions and put in all efforts for the sake of productivity (Bhowon, 2001). Mauritius has been experiencing significant structural changes in its economy and in 2015, active women represented 47% of the female population aged 16 years and above (Republic of Mauritius Report, 2015). *"We cannot build a world which is liveable if it walks only on one foot— continuing to neglect, by obscure prejudices, 50 percent of the talent, skill, and energy available."* (A.Z. de Thuin, President and Founder, The Women's Forum for the Economy and Society).

After independence, successive governments have taken the commitment to promote gender equality and improving women's standard of living and quality of life. Bold initiatives have been taken by investing in health, education, institutional mechanisms, economic empowerment and poverty alleviation programmes which have been instrumental to the acceleration of equality between men and women to ensure

The Contribution of Women Towards Nation-Building... 169

that all international and regional commitments pertaining to women's empowerment and the promotion of gender equality were effectively transformed into policies and programmes and that these did not remain just declarations of intent. Mauritius has made significant progress towards achieving gender equality and promoting the well- being of women and the government is fully committed to transforming the country into an inclusive, high-income country by 2030. Several measures and strategies are being put in place to enhance inclusive growth and among are the increase of female labour participation from 43.6% currently to 50% by 2030 (HRDC Report, 2017).

The increasing contribution of women is highly noticeable in various spheres of the economy. Over the last two decades, they have shifted from the agricultural sector to the manufacturing sector and now are in the service sector. Nowadays, the country is currently moving towards expanding the tertiary sector, more specifically the service sector. Moreover, sectors like agro-industry have diversified to agro-processing activities (MAIFS, 2016). Today, women are well represented in different sectors, such as education, medicine, dentistry, managerial positions as well as clerical jobs. However, according to the Equal Opportunity Commission Report 2014, the Mauritian women are more vulnerable to some forms of discrimination at work. Studies on women in developing countries have indicated that women in developing countries undertake a 'triple role' because of their contribution to unpaid domestic duties with paid employment as well as community management activities (Moser, 1993).

The factors which affect women's professional role in a patriarchal society are mainly pregnancy, maternity leave, marital status and family responsibilities. The main purpose of this qualitative study is to find out the perceptions of young Mauritian females on the contribution of women into making Mauritius a success story. The research questions were:

170   *Diaspora and Nation-Building*

- To what extent do Mauritian women contribute to nation-building?
- Do the women function effectively in the modern economic system?
- What were the difficulties women experience in their role performance towards nation-building?

  Purposive sampling was used and fifteen in-depth face-to-face interviews were conducted among young Mauritian women between ages of 18 and 26 years old. They were from different backgrounds and professions in different sectors, ranging from the textile industry, clerical, teaching, managerial positions to dentistry and medicine. The main sections of the interviews were

- Mauritian women contribute to nation-building
- Role of Mauritian women in the economy
- Difficulties women experience in their role performance towards nation-building

In this study, the ethics was fully respected. Suitable explanations were given to the respondents about the motive of the study. All interviewees were asked for their consent beforehand by the use of a consent form (Appendix B). A request letter and testimonial were also provided for acknowledgement and access. The responses and identity of respondents were kept private and confidential where only the researcher had access. Overall, the research ensured a safe environment to the participants.

Most participants agreed on the fact that women do contribute to the economy in a positive way. Some of their testimonies are:

"When more women work, economies grow!

It is high time to acknowledge women's contribution in the economy.

Empowering women to participate equally in the global economy adds to our GDP.

The Contribution of Women Towards Nation-Building... 171

However, while Mauritius has made significant progress towards achieving gender equality and promoting well-being of women, there is still ample room for improvement. Some of the respondent's arguments are that even though women represent more than 52% of the Mauritian population, *women are still the ones who interrupt their careers to handle the requirements of their family life, usually because of the absence of a support system to help them balance both aspects.*

Just like women's visible work is the household, women's work in the community-building often goes unacknowledged.

Women have always been the backbone to a nation's growth but they continue to face systemic barriers and frustrations in the workplace.

Women remain under-represented in business leadership roles.

They face discrimination and are victims of glass ceiling:

Thus, among the difficulties faced by some Mauritian women are mainly:

Discrimination and equal pay

Despite the laws and policies supporting women's economic empowerment in Mauritius, inequalities of wages and incomes between men and women continue to prevail. Discrepancies occur because more women are engaged in lower skilled jobs and, consequently, lower paid jobs than men. Women also form the majority of unemployed in the country. In terms of income, women's average earnings are lower than men's in all of the sectors. The differences are more pronounced in the agricultural sector, elementary occupations and in retail. Given that the laws in the country render sex discrimination illegal, men and women are entitled to the same salaries, based on experience and qualifications. Differences arise at the levels of skills and types of job. In the public sectors, there is a slight difference in the average monthly income between men and women. This would be

172   *Diaspora and Nation-Building*

due to the fact that more men than women occupy the higher positions that command a higher salary.

- **Gender violence including domestic violence**

Women are most likely to be victims of domestic violence. In 2015, out of 1,626 new cases of domestic violence registered at the Ministry of Gender Equality, Child Development and Family Welfare, nearly 89 percent were against women. Over the past five years, domestic violence against women has been declining slightly. Some 24 percent of women victims of domestic violence reported physical assault by spouse or partner, 14 percent verbal assault by spouse or partners (ill-treatment, harassment, abuse and humiliation), 12 percent threatening assault by spouse and an equal proportion has been subjected to harassment by spouse (Gender Situation Analysis in the Republic of Mauritius, 2016).

Culture factor pertaining to our patriarchal society

Triple responsibilities on women

63% of women respondents are agreeable that long working hours will mean a sacrifice to their family time. This in itself represents a big hurdle, since women already struggle with their triple roles as wife, mother and the woman in society.

In Mauritius, women tend to spend more time on non-market economic activities than men. Although data that is more recent is not available, the time use survey carried out by Statistics Mauritius in 2003 revealed the following:

- Women spent about 116 minutes per day in market economic activities, whereas men spent 296 minutes per day in these activities.
- The unaccounted contribution of men to the economy as a percentage of the Gross Domestic Product (GDP) of market price lies in the range of 3.9% to 6.6% while that of women is almost three times more, in

The Contribution of Women Towards Nation-Building... 173

the higher range of 11.3% to 24.1%.

- The average woman spends 314 minutes per day on unpaid work, i.e., four times more than the average of 80 minutes for the average man.
- Mothers are spending four to five times more than fathers on household work. Only paid employment and the exchange of commodities for money is registered as part of the GDP in national accounting systems. The contribution of women to the national economy is, therefore, underestimated.

However, Mauritius has ratified several international human rights instruments, which also cover women's rights and are conducive to gender equality. Prominent among these are the Convention on the Elimination of All Forms of Discrimination against Women (CEDAW), which was ratified by Mauritius in 1984. Mauritius endorsed the Beijing Declaration and Platform for Action (BPFA) in 1995. Mauritius also ratified the Optional Protocol on Violence against Women in 2008 and the Protocol to the African Charter on Human and Peoples' Rights on the Rights of Women in Africa in 2005. The Constitution of Mauritius enshrines a philosophy of equality and reforms in the laws of the country have ensured that women have the same legal rights as men. As such, everybody is equal before the law and nobody can be discriminated against, directly or indirectly, on grounds including age, sex, creed, ethnicity or even religion.

On a conclusive note, it can be said that indeed women are the backbone of the Mauritian society. With the inclusion of women in different spheres of development ranging from economic, social to political, the country will continue to make striking progress and grow productivity.

Notes and References

1. Bela, A.M. (1998) Women and Men in the Maltese Islands. Statistics from the Census of Population and Housing.

174   *Diaspora and Nation-Building*

Valletta: Department for Women's Rights, Ministry for Social Policy

2. Allen, Priscilla, Women and Work: A Perspective from the United States Female Labor Force Participation: 'Impact on Labor Productivity and Economic Growth' conference paper at the Asian Productivity Organisation (Tokyo, 5-7 April 2016)

3. Asian Development Bank. 2010. Proposed Grant to the Lao People's Democratic Republic: Strengthening Technical and Vocational Education and Training Project. Manila. Bezzina, C & Dibben, A. (2002) Bittersweet: Living as a Young Unmarried Mother. Unpublished B.A. (Hons) in Social Work, University of Malta, Msida. Bhowon, Uma, Role Salience, 'Work-Family Conflict and Satisfaction of Dual-Earner Couples', Journal of Business Studies Quarterly.

4. Boserup, E., 1971, Women's role in economic development, George, Allen and Unwin Ltd. London.

5. Brocas, A., Cailloux, A. and Oget, V. (1990) Women and Social Security. Progress Towards Equality of Treatment. Geneva: International Labour Office.

6. Cain, G.G. (1966). Labour Force Participation of Married Women. Chicago: University of Chicago Press.

7. Constitution of Mauritius (1968).

8. Cutajar, J.A. (2000) Widowhood in the Island where Time Stands Still: Gender, Ethnicity and Citizenship in the Maltese Islands. Unpublished Ph.D. in Sociology and Equity Studies in Education, University of Toronto, Canada.

9. Fujimura, Hiroyuki, 'Female Labor Force Participation Trends and Patterns: Research findings from APO countries, conference paper at the Asian Productivity Organisation' (Tokyo, 5-7 the April 2016)

10. Gender Links, Study on Gender Analysis in the Republic of Mauritius (2016).

11. Goldin, C., 1986, 'The Economic Status of Women in the Early Republic: Quantitative Evidence', The Journal of Interdisciplinary History, 16:3. pp. 375-404.

12. Hanson, S. and Pratt, G. (1995) Gender, Work and Space. London: Routledge.

13. Heuveline, P., Timberlake, J.M. & Furstenberg, F.F. (2003)

The Contribution of Women Towards Nation-Building... 175

'Shifting Childrearing to Single Mothers: Results from 17 Western Countries'. Population and Development Review. Vol. 29, No. 1, Pp. 47-71.

14. International Labour Organisation. 2004. Gender Equality and Decent Work: Good Practices at the Workplace. Geneva: pp. 31–35.

15. International Labour Organisation. 2006. Decent Work for Women and Men in the Informal Economy: Profile and Good Practices in Cambodia. Bangkok and Phnom Penh. p. 56–57.

16. J.F. Illo (ed). 2010. Accounting for Gender Results. A Review of the Philippine GAD Budget Policy. Miriam College. Manila: 117; R. Sharp, D. Elson, M.

17. Kember, M. (1997) 'Women and Education. Introduction', in C. Ungerson& M. Kember (eds.) Women and Social Policy. A Reader. (Pp. 233-237). London: Macmillan.

18. Labour Force, Employment and Unemployment, Statistics, Mauritius (2016)

19. M. A. Chen, J. Vanek, and M. Carr. 2004. Mainstreaming Informal Employment and Gender in Poverty Reduction. London: Commonwealth Secretariat, Ottawa: International Development Research Centre (IDRC) and Women in Informal Employment: Globalizing and Organising. p. 129. 46. Mauritius Millennium Development Goals (2015).

20. Mauritius National Budget (2017-2018).

21. Mincer, Jacob (1962): 'Labour Force Participation of Married Women: A Study of Labour Supply'; Aspects of Labour Economics – A Conference of the Universities: National Bureau Committee for Economic Research, Princeton University Press, NJ, USA.

22. Mitra, Arup, 'Government Policy to Enhance FLFP', conference paper at the Asian Productivity Organisation (Tokyo, 5-7 the April 2016)

23. MTCI (2015) ICT Penetration in Private Household Indicators.

24. National version of the International Standard Classification of Occupations (ISCO-08) Negotiating the new complexities of trade: An analysis of the feminisation of informal sector workers poverty in Mauritius, Research paper, Asrani Gopaul.

176   *Diaspora and Nation-Building*

25. National Youth Policy, Ministry of Youth and Sports (2016).
26. UN Sustainable Development 2016 Report.
27. UN Women, 2015, Facts and Figures: Economic Empowerment.
28. UNDP Country Office of Mauritius, Gender Briefing Kit for the Republic of Mauritius (2013).
29. Women's Economic Empowerment, The OECD DAC Network on Gender Equality (GENDERNET, 2011) https://www.oecd.org/dac/povertyreduction/50157530.pdf.
30. World Economic Forum, 2017, Accelerating Gender Parity in the fourth Industrial Revolution.
31. Yuko Kinoshita and Fang Guo, What Can Boost Female Labor Force Participation in Asia, IMF Working Paper (2015) https://www.imf.org/external/pubs/ft/wp/2015/wp1556.pdf.

□

Closing Statement by D.G, MGI & RTI

—*Mrs. Sooryakanti Nirsimloo-Gayan*

I would like to say that it is 3 o'clock on a Friday afternoon. And you probably don't wish me to be talking for too long. But as one of the co-hosts of the conference, I felt, I had a duty to say a few words and perhaps share with you a few thoughts about what might be topics of interest for the future with respect to research in this field of 'diaspora'.

First of all, echoing perhaps some of the observations that have been said by our friends from Reunion Island, I would like to suggest that one area that deserves to be looked into much more closely is the migration that took place in the Indian Ocean between Mauritius and Reunion Island, and between Mauritius and the Seychelles. In particular, there are possibilities of conducting case studies of concrete experiences of migration after the Second World War from Mauritius to Reunion Island, experiences of settlement that transformed significant aspects of cultural and religious life among people of Indian descent in Reunion Island. This connect is a very recent one, but is not sufficiently documented. The phenomenon is worth looking into as it can throw light on second migration and even third migrant communities, which carried with them an amount of cultural baggage that is absolutely mind-blowing even to this day.

178   *Diaspora and Nation-Building*

Secondly, a word about the concept of Diaspora. Diaspora starts off in a very circumscribed manner when it comes to experience of the Jewish Diaspora, and as regards the Greek origin of the word. And yet, it has come to embrace a very diverse and contrasted set of migration experiences. So, I ask myself whether it is not time to start engaging afresh with the word 'Diaspora' and perhaps looking at how our grasp of this multi-faceted concept might be transformed. Looking through theories of complexity and theories of complex organisations and embracing them adds different dimensions of cross-cultural flows.

And, of course, a lot is being said about trans-national communities, but again, I think all these terms do not quite yet capture this variety, this range and this amazing transformative power that migration has represented throughout the 20th and 21st centuries.

In addition, as Sri Gupta was saying, at the opening ceremony yesterday, the Indian migration experience has profoundly impacted on the way host communities perceive migrant populations. This deserves to be looked into more closely. What is the cultural baggage, what is the profile, psychological and emotional; that these people carry with them that make the experience somewhat different from the experiences of other migrant communities around the world?

And, then, the fourth point which comes to my mind is the question of what happens to heritage. 'Diaspora' is laden with 'heritage'. But what happens to heritage when you have policy-makers, policy organisations taking over from individuals or communities the function of preservation? We have, for example in Mauritius Le Morne, which has been inscribed on UNESCO's World Heritage List. Same goes for Aapravasi Ghat. Following the inscription, there is a management component that comes into play. There is a policy of preservation, of promotion, of development which has taken over. This, in a way, has become the relay from what had been taking

Closing Statement by D.G, MGI & RTI 179

place at community level and, in some cases, even at very, very individual levels, where people devoted themselves, volunteered to keep alive the tangible and intangible marks of history. Now, when the state and policy-makers take over, what happens at the level of the community in terms of perception, and in terms of engagement and commitment?

Fifth, if I may, let me have a special word about Bollywood, because Bollywood has made a tremendous difference to the global Indian Diaspora and it has gone beyond, way beyond anything we could have imagined or foreseen. I still remember, when I was a child, going to see an Indian movie was an absolutely central experience of entertainment. There were a few cinema halls that showed Indian films and the Indian High Commission in Mauritius also had a mobile cinema unit that travelled from village to village, showing documentaries and feature films. All this has been part of the process of keeping alive the connection as well, and deserves to be talked about and shared with young people.

One thought about the cultural baggage. A lot is said precisely about the way the Indian communities adapt and engage in a peaceful, in a very pacifist manner, in countries where they settle.

And I wonder, today, when the emphasis is on commerce, on trade, where there is hard bargaining – what is there in the cultural values, in terms of ethics, in terms of honesty, that Indian diasporas may still be able to draw from in order to make a difference much more broadly in their adopted lands?

We tend to lose sight of this heritage once we are sucked into the market mechanics. We lose sight of the fact that there are values that have to underpin the marketplace as well.

A few weeks ago, I had the opportunity of having some conversations with young students of Mahatma Gandhi Secondary Schools. I am referring to a group of adolescents. Two of them asked me whether the Nation, the Mauritian nation was a myth. They seemed to be a little concerned

180 *Diaspora and Nation-Building*

about this possibility. And so, we spent some time trying to demystify 'the Nation'. Not that I did it too well, I was probably very clumsy, but we were trying to demystify on the one hand, the Mauritian nation and, on the other hand, we were asking ourselves whether it was such a bad thing if it were a myth.

And, in a way, when I look at the title of this conference *'Contribution of Diaspora to Nation Building'*, I have a feeling that we are talking about one myth, Diaspora, contributing to the construction of another myth, the Nation.

I do not say this negatively at all because I ask myself: "where is hope if there is no myth to believe in?"

So, I shall end with this – that we have to believe in our nation, but we also have to believe in that diasporic identity, which contributes to our own individual sense of being.

Thank you.

□

Statement by Hon. Minister of Tourism, Republic of Mauritius

—Shri Anil Kumarsingh Gayan

I am deeply honoured to have been invited by the Antar-Rashtriya Sahayog Parishad (ARSP) to participate in the valedictory session of this very important event intended to promote the influence of the Indian Diaspora in nation-building and the socio-economic development of Mauritius.

I wish to acknowledge the contribution of ARSP in promoting the ancestral world view of India, i.e. 'Vasudhaiva Kutumbakam', which means 'the whole world is one family'.

We are particularly pleased that Mauritius has been chosen as the venue for this International Conference with the theme 'Contribution of Indian Diaspora in Nation-Building'. We are happier that the event coincides with the 50th anniversary of our independence, which has such a historical significance for all communities. In fact, you may wish to know that whenever there was a Hindu wedding in the past, the flag that was made to fly was the Indian flag. At present, it is the Mauritian flag that is proudly displayed, although the occasional Indian flag is also put up. This shows that the transition to a nationhood is well under way. A nation develops an identity with time and this is even more time-consuming in a multi-ethnic country like ours.

182   *Diaspora and Nation-Building*

From the outline of your Programme, I can see that this two-day Conference has explored at length the different stages and facets of the contribution of the Indian diaspora in building modern Mauritius, as well as the role that diaspora has played and continues to play in nation-building in all those countries where Indians went to settle. A number of key issues have been addressed, such as democracy, modernisation, education and technology. I am sure the discussions on these matters have been rich, and will prompt you to pursue further deliberations on these highly engaging topics. I must here strike a word of caution. States have their own interests and it would be wrong to address the issues relating to the diaspora in a romantic way and to consider only cultural and religious aspects of the diaspora engagements. An adult approach of diaspora engagement is required to understand the role of diaspora in state and nation-building.

India has been extremely generous in its policy of free movement of its people. Over the years, more than 30 million members of the Indian diaspora have settled in more than one hundred countries. They have settled to a large extent successfully and developed a sense of belonging, whilst maintaining their cultural heritage and upholding their values and beliefs.

The historical importance of the labour diaspora for the Indian Ocean region as a whole is that it was the largest movement of population to take place in this part of the world during the 19th and early 20th century. Between 1834 and 1924, more than 454,000 labourers were recruited in India and brought to the Mauritian shores. More than two-thirds of them remained on the island, redefining the social, demographic, economic, religious and political landscape of the country.

There is a growing international recognition of the importance of the diaspora in the quest for identity and cultural legacy. Many countries have schemes to cultivate links

Statement by Hon. Minister of Tourism, Republic of Mauritius 183

with their diaspora and some countries even have Ministries and diplomats designated specifically to handle diaspora affairs. The diaspora is a prime example of the influence of 'soft power'.

Let me say one thing about how India is reinforcing this linkage. The Overseas Citizen of India (OCI) Card is a bond between India and the Diaspora. But questions may be asked about the limitations imposed by the OCI Card? The limitations are the ineligibility to vote in elections and the prohibition to purchase farm land. This illustrates the conflict between the State and the diaspora. The issues of citizenship and sovereignty overlap, and at times it is impossible to reconcile full citizenship to the diaspora. Nothing stops India to revisit these limitations bearing in mind that very few people would take advantage of full citizenship.

China has a special arrangement, whereby persons of Chinese origin are co-opted to sit as members of the Legislature. France has a number of seats in Parliament reserved for overseas French people. India could consider such an arrangement to consolidate the process of bonding.

There are certain issues which people from the diaspora raise about the role of India. The basis of international relations is the recognition of sovereignty of states and the principle of non-interference in the domestic affairs of another State. Let me illustrate how these issues are raised. In Fiji, the Indian – origin Prime Minister, Mahendra Chowdhury was overturned by a military coup. Could India have done something about that? Should India have done something about that? Could, for example, India have led an international effort to support the democratically elected Prime Minister?

The second issue I want to raise is the plight of all Asians who were expelled by the dictator of Uganda, Idi Amin Dada, in the early 1970s. What could India have done to come to the help of the Asian Ugandans? Today those Asians who went to the United Kingdom are among the wealthiest Britons.

184 *Diaspora and Nation-Building*

I do not have answers to these issues but, with the rise of India as a growing economic and military power, we may explore new ways of meeting the concerns of the Indian diaspora in respecting international correctness.

Africa will emerge as the continent of the future. With immeasurable natural resources and a young population coupled with increasing prosperity, it is now wonder that China has been engaged there for centuries. The China – Africa Forum is a major event for the calendar of the African Presidents and Heads of Governments. India has waded in with a similar event. India must avoid the pitfalls of China in Africa and engage with Africans in a spirit of shared values and interests. India has the advantage of democracy and the English language. These are non-negligible assets for Africans. Opening higher education institutions in India to Africans will enhance its influence over those who will eventually become the leaders and elite of their respective countries. The former Soviet Union did it, China is doing it now and India would be well advised to follow. Shaping the minds of future African leaders is within India's reach.

As we are all aware, Mauritius has nurtured a special relationship with India and all governments since independence. The frequent high-level visits and the programme of assistance in many areas are testimony to the quality of this special relationship. We respect each other as sovereign nations but, whenever one country needs the other, every effort is made to meet that need.

Mauritius has always extolled the virtue of a diplomacy which has prioritised a policy of friends to all. We take pride in our multicultural and multiethnic heritage and are widely considered an example of tolerance among various communities, religions and cultures. There are not many places in the world where such diversity is concentrated in such a small area. Within a radius of few hundred metres,

Statement by Hon. Minister of Tourism, Republic of Mauritius 185

we can find a Hindu temple, a mosque, a pagoda, a Christian church and other religious shrines. The contribution of each and every community to our socio-economic development continues to be valued and celebrated.

As Minister of Tourism, my philosophy is that tourism contributes overwhelmingly to building alliances among people from different backgrounds and cultures. Tourism is, therefore, the prime example of people-to-people diplomacy. Similarly, the diaspora also has an important role to play in promoting diplomacy so that people's relations can prosper. It is against this backdrop that I make an appeal to our diaspora around the world to give back to the country of origin in whichever way possible.

Connecting with the ancestral land takes many forms in this modern world. There is no corner of India that cannot be accessed through the Internet.

Having said this, I would like to end on a note of thanks to the ARSP for putting together this event with all the local stakeholders at such an opportune moment. We look forward to welcoming you again to Mauritius in the near future for more fruitful collaboration.

☐

Statement by H.E The President, Republic of Mauritius

—Mr. Paramasivum Pillay Vyapoory, GOSK

It is indeed a great pleasure and honour for me to participate in the valedictory session of this International Conference on the theme "Contribution of Indian Diaspora in Nation-Building: Mauritius—a Case Study". Let me first extend a personal hearty welcome to scholars and delegates from abroad and I am sure that during these two days, you have been able to fathom the extent to which the Indian diaspora in Mauritius has contributed to building the nation, Our Nation.

As we know, India has the largest diaspora in the world with more than 31 million people of Indian origin spread across about 110 countries. In most cases across the world, the Non Resident Indians (NRIs) have proved to be assets for their countries of adoption and have contributed to the economic development of their new countries. During a visit to the United States, Prime Minister Modi heaped praise on the Indian diaspora and credited it for lifting India's image in the world with the following words, I quote, *"Your fingers created magic on the keyboard of the computer and this gave India a new identity. Your skill and commitment are wonderful."*

Today, the world is more globalised, interconnected and interdependent than ever before. The recent global economic crisis shows us that it is no longer possible for any nation state

Statement by H.E The President, Republic of Mauritius   187

to consider itself an 'island', nor it is possible to be immune from the ebbs and flows of global economics. In order to be in a position to fully leverage the advantages of interdependence, companies, organisations and countries are looking at creating, developing and engaging complex networks of people to generate social, cultural and economic benefits.

Diasporas constitute obvious collectives of people through which networks can be created and individuals can be mobilised for mutual benefit. Traditionally, we looked at diasporas through the looking glass of remittances and financial flows which, now, is to take a myopic view. Diasporas are a bridge to knowledge, expertise, resources and markets for the country of origin.

In the case of Mauritius, our ancestors came to the island from India, mostly in the early to mid-19th century as artisans, construction workers and indentured labourers for the sugar estates. These labourers left the Indian subcontinent from a variety of ports, and so reflected the diversity of India itself. The first contingent of Indian immigrants to Mauritius was during the French occupation when thousands left the port of Madras for Mauritius as artisans and construction workers. They helped to build the capital, Port Louis – the harbour, the Post Office, the hospital, schools and roads.

When as indentured labourers, our *girmitiya* grandfathers and great grandfathers climbed the flight of 16 steps of the Aapravasi Ghat on 2 November 1834, they had a vision, mainly to pave the way for a better future for their descendants. The story of the *girmitiyas* is one of the immense struggles and sufferings. But it is also one of the most inspirational chapters of Mauritian history. The *girmitiyas* struggled with dignity and perseverance, and through sheer determination and hard work, they eventually triumphed – a triumph of the human spirit in the face of terrible adversity.

The visit of Mahatma Gandhi to Mauritius in 1901 on his way from South Africa to India provided a wake-up call to the

188 *Diaspora and Nation-Building*

Indian immigrants. Mahatma Gandhi held meetings with the opinion leaders of Mauritius and convinced them that their emancipation for justice resides in them getting involved in politics and giving importance to education especially for the young ones. These pieces of advice did not fall on deaf ears. And to give concrete expression to his words, Gandhi sent Manilall Doctor. The latter successfully inculcated the interest in politics and education in the mind of Mauritians. His work was continued by pundits like Professor Basdeo Bissoondoyal, Permal Soobrayen and others.

On the political field, Sir Seewoosagur Ramgoolam rose up as a leader with very able support from Renganaden Seeneevassen, Razack Mohamed, Sookdeo Bissoondayal and many others. Trade Union leaders rose to the challenge and Anjalay Coopen became a martyr along with 3 other labourers in the fight for basic human rights. Successive generations have played their part. Many leaders have emerged – Sir Veerasamy Ringadoo, Sir Satcam Boolell, on the political field. Sir Seewoosagur Ramgoolam, the father of the Nation was the first Prime Minister. Successive Prime Ministers were Sir Anerood Jugnauth, Paul Berenger, Navin Ramgoolam and, presently, the youngest Prime Minister in the person of Pravind Kumar Jugnauth.

Since their first landing in Mauritius, the Indian immigrants never relinquish their attachment to Indian culture, Indian values and their religion. In spite of waves of influence to conversion, the great majority of Indian immigrants kept practising and living their culture through organising religious and cultural festivals like Mahashivaratri, Cavadee, Ganesh Chaturthi, Ugadi, Eid, Sankranti, Diwali and others.

The setting up of institutions like the Mahatma Gandhi Institute, the Indira Gandhi Centre for Indian Culture, the Rabindranath Tagore Institute, the Swami Vivekananda International Convention Centre, the Rajiv Gandhi Science

Statement by H.E The President, Republic of Mauritius 189

Centre and, recently, various Cultural Centre Trusts and Speaking Unions have largely contributed to keep Indian Culture and the Indian way of life alive in Mauritius. Indian languages are taught at all levels of education in Mauritius. Indian films are also very popular and coupled with radio programmes with songs, news and information in the various Indian languages also contribute to making of Mauritius a little India.

The sons and daughters of successive generations have given great importance to education. As qualified professionals they serve in the nation-building process. If from a low-income country with a monocrop economy, Mauritius has graduated over the 50 years since independence in 1968 to an upper middle income economy, aspiring to rise to a high-income economy, it is definitely thanks to the role of the Indian diaspora along with that of the other ethnic groups.

I shall conclude by congratulating the organisers and delegates of this International Conference which I am sure have been very fruitful. I look forward to take cognizance of your resolutions which definitely will aim towards enhancing the coexistence of descendants of our grandfathers and great grandfathers coming from India.

□

Vote of Thanks

—Shri Shyam Parande

The opening session:

It is my privilege to propose a vote of thanks.

I would like to thank The Rt. Hon. Sir Anerood Jugnauth, former Prime Minister and, currently, Minister Mentor for giving the keynote address. Sir, your speech was inspiring and will guide us in our future endeavour. Listening to a leader of your stature is always a great education as it flows from personal experience; there could be no better account of the Mauritian history and of the relationship between our two countries and peoples.

We received extraordinary support from the Mauritian Ministry of Art and Culture and feel obliged that Minister Mr. Prithvirajsing Roopun could spare his valuable time to attend and address the opening session. It was indeed a treat to watch him trace through the history of Mauritius and the role of diaspora at every stage of the nation-building process.

This conference would not have been possible without the unwavering support we have received from our partners and co-hosts, the Mahatma Gandhi Institute (MGI) and the Aapravasi Ghat Trust Fund (AGTF) and our sincere gratitude goes to Mr. Jaynarain Meetoo, Chairman, MGI and Mr. Dharam Yash Deo Dhuny, Chairman, AGTF. Both Mr. Meetoo and Mr. Dhuny have been personal witnesses to important stages in

Vote of Thanks

Mauritian history and of the success story of Apravasis of Indian origin. MGI and AGTF are the true custodian of this heritage and have preserved it with passion and perfection. We are deeply touched by their support and goodwill.

The valedictory session:

If we were privileged to have the guidance of The Rt. Hon. Sir Anerood Jugnauth at the inaugural session, we feel exceptionally fortunate to have the gracious presence of the acting President of Mauritius, HE Paramasivum Pillay Vyapoory to weigh the outcomes and lay an effective roadmap into the future. Excellency, we are so moved by your words of support and appreciation for what this conference could contribute in bringing our two countries and people closer. We are so encouraged that we would return back to India with much greater confidence and trust that our relationship transcends beyond conventional considerations.

Hon. Mr. Anil Kumarsing Gayan, Minister of Tourism, we are thankful to you for sparing your valuable time for addressing the valedictory session in your usual frank and down-to-earth style. Sir, that is what we were looking for. You were also very kind to host a dinner for all the participants and we shall remember this great gesture dearly.

Our special gratitude goes to Mrs. Gayan, DG, MGI for such wonderful support. The idea of this Conference was, in fact, first discussed with her at our conference in New Delhi. Her assurance of support gave us the courage and confidence to undertake this important and challenging initiative.

The technical sessions deliberated on the relevant themes with depth and frankness. The discussions generated a wealth of knowledge and ideas. I would like to extend my sincere gratitude to all the speakers for making these sessions so thought-provoking.

I would also like to give my sincere gratitude to the High Commissioner of India in Mauritius and his team for their

192   *Diaspora and Nation-Building*

excellent support and arrangement for successfully organising this conference.

The conference was covered live by Mauritius Broadcasting Corporation. The print media also carried several reports and articles. I would like to express my gratitude to them.

Finally, our appreciation for the organising teams from MGI, AGTF and ARSP (DRRC) for an outstanding choreography of the events.

❑

Summary Report of the Conference (Mauritius)

—Amb. Anup K. Mudgal

Antar Rashtriya Sahayog Parishad (ARSP), New Delhi organised a two-day International Conference in Mauritius on 5th-6th July, 2018 on the topic: 'Contribution of Diaspora in Nation-Building' in partnership with the Aapravasi Ghat Trust Fund (AGTF) and Mahatma Gandhi Institute (MGI) from Mauritius, and in collaboration with the PIO Chamber of Commerce and Industry, (PIOCCI), New Delhi. The conference was organised in continuation of the ARSP's year-long commemoration of the centenary of the abolition of the Indentured system and as a part of the celebrations to mark the fiftieth anniversary year of the Mauritian independence.

The conference discussed the role of diaspora in nation-building, providing a comprehensive perspective from their history to the contemporary developments in political, economic and socio-cultural fields as also their future vision. Besides the formal opening and closing sessions, the conference had five technical sessions to develop various themes, namely (i) Independence movements and political developments – establishment and working of the democratic institutions; (ii) Economic Development and modernisation;

194   *Diaspora and Nation-Building*

(iii) Socio-cultural experience, including higher education and technology; and (iv) Role of diaspora in nation-building-the Mauritian experience. There was a fifth session which was kept open for discussing any aspect not covered by the structured sessions.

The conference generated serious interest not only amongst the academicians and scholars, but equally among the political/diplomatic community and media, as such a wide-ranging and contemporary theme was seen in full sync with the growing sense of pride and confidence in the members of Indian diaspora. They are no more limited to seeking quality jobs, good education or business opportunities, but are aiming much higher in terms of a larger role in nation-building. They are no more hesitant to take a plunge into the local political developments. While in the countries of the Indentured Route, the Indian diaspora has historically been an integral part of the nation-building process, their much wider foot-print was evident when around 150 PIO Parliamentarians and Mayors from over 20 countries attended the first-ever conference of PIO Parliamentarians and Mayors, hosted by the Government of India in January this year.

Some two dozen academics, experts and former civil servants dealing with diaspora issues participated from India and an equal number joined the deliberations from Mauritius on various themes. We also had a few participants from Reunion, Trinidad and Tobago, Malaysia and Singapore. In addition, several members of MGI faculty and local scholars attended various sessions of their interest.

The Inaugural session at the Subramaniam Auditorium of MGI, packed to capacity, was chaired by legendary The Right Hon'ble Sir Anerood Jugnauth, who had served the highest offices as Head of State and Head of Government for over

Summary Report of the Conference (Mauritius) 195

two decades of the Mauritian post independence period and currently the Minister mentor. At present, he is the senior-most Mauritian leader and Statesman. He was accompanied by Lady Jugnauth to the function. Hon. Mr. Prithvirajsing Roopum, Minister of Culture was the guest of honour, whereas the Chairperson of MGI/RTI Mr. Jaynarain Meetoo and the Chairperson of AGTF, Mr. Dhahran Yash Deo Dhuny were also present to grace the occasion.

Minister Roopun traced the history of Mauritius and the contribution of diaspora not only in the independence struggle, but also the post-independence building of nation. He highlighted the high democratic standard Mauritius had achieved by respecting individual liberties and its rich diversity, while at the same time turning the Mauritian economy from backward mono-crop based low income to knowledge-driven high middle-income economy. Similar accounts were narrated by the Chairpersons of MGI and AGTF on educational, cultural and technology fronts.

The highlight of the opening ceremony was the inaugural address by the Rt. Hon. Sir Anerood Jugnauth where he fondly recalled the function when he laid the foundation stone of the ARSP headquarters in New Delhi, and appreciated the excellent work done by the organisation for promoting the diaspora's welfare and closer engagement with India and the Indian culture. He also thanked the valuable support provided by India at various stages of Mauritian development. Sir Jugnauth credited the Indian values of tolerance, hard work, sacrifice and perseverance to have been at the heart of the Mauritian model of inclusive development. Mauritian economy is driven by knowledge, skills and innovation.

The conference culminated with an equally impressive valedictory which was presided over by the acting President

196 *Diaspora and Nation-Building*

of Mauritius, HE Paramasivum Pillay Vyapoory, whereas the Minister of Tourism, Hon. Mr. Anil Kumarsing Gayan attended as the guest of honour. President recalled the democratic and syncretism values which the Indian diaspora has carried with them to far off places in the world. He appreciated the bridge-building role of diaspora in bringing the communities closer with greater mutual understanding and appreciation. President also underlined the contribution of Mauritian leaders of Indian descent in the nation-building process, especially Sir Seewoosagur Ramgoolam, Anerood Jugnauth and others. He also appreciated various initiatives of the GOI in encouraging diaspora's constructive engagement with India and their Indian routes.

Minister Gayan also retraced the historic contributions of diaspora in the nation-building process in Mauritius and praised various efforts of GOI in protecting the interests of diaspora. He sought more measures for closer and enhanced engagement with India, including in the process of policy formulation and execution. He said, the diaspora was a stakeholder in the Indian development and performance, and there should be more channels to enable them play this role.

The four technical sessions deliberated on the relevant themes with greater depth and full frankness.

The conference was covered live by Mauritius Broadcasting Corporation. The print media also carried several reports and articles.

Minister Gayan went out of way to host a formal dinner for all the visiting delegates. Another goodwill dinner was hosted by the Human Service Trust, which has been the breeding ground of Mauritian political philosophy and leadership.

While the MGI provided the venue and the organisational support, the AGTF made other local arrangements.

Summary Report of the Conference (Mauritius)   197

The conference produced a series of ideas and recommendations for further strengthening India's engagement with its diaspora as also to support the diaspora in developing greater capacity for nation-building in their adopted countries for building more effective bridges of understanding between them and India. Some of the key recommendations are summarised below for further follow up:

(a) While the biannual PBD process does provide a high-level platform to discuss and address the diaspora issues, there is a need for a more interactive permanent global consultative mechanism for dealing with diaspora needs in more real-term manner. This could be channelled through a connected and coordinated network of non-governmental diaspora organisations. With its experience and goodwill, ARSP could play an important role in this regard.

(b) To explore some permanent and reliable channel of dialogue between the diaspora and the Indian policy-making bodies so that the diaspora issues and opinion could be better integrated with the evolving policy in a more effective manner.

(c) Better arrangements for teaching Indian languages abroad, especially for diaspora children so that they are able to better connect with their cultural routes.

(d) There is a compelling need for engaging the diaspora youth by way of education, skill development, trade, investment and employment. This becomes more pressing as the diaspora plays a greater role in nation-building in their adopted societies. Better-equipped, empowered, skilled and connected

198   *Diaspora and Nation-Building*

youth diaspora would provide a more effective and sustainable bridge between India and their adopted countries.

(e) Members of diaspora educated in India rose to occupy important positions in various spheres of influence in their adopted countries. This was particularly true of the *girmitiya* societies and the new-age diaspora centres. With the changing situation of educational needs, quality, cost and spending capacity, the earlier preference for India as a destination for higher studies is declining. Diaspora youth are becoming more exacting in their demands for better courses and institutions. In the recent years, there has been a visible fall in diaspora seeking admissions in Indian institutions of higher education. This needs to be reversed through a comprehensive review of India's scholarships programme.

(f) The need for setting up of centres for diaspora studies. With the growing size and importance of diaspora, there should be a suitable inclusion of diaspora studies in schools and college curriculum. ARSP's initiative to set up Diaspora Documentation and Research Centre is a good step in that direction.

(g) There is a need for greater cultural outreach for not so well known diaspora centres like Reunion lest they are left completely disconnected.

(h) Address the glitches of the OCI system to establish Indian origin with removal of caps on number of generations, especially in the *girmitiya* countries. The changes made for Mauritian national in the OCI

Summary Report of the Conference (Mauritius) 199

eligibility criteria was a welcome step and similar solutions should be explored for other countries. One fit-all approach is not effective in resolving specific problems.

The conference ended with a resolve to continue with such consultative process with greater vigour and regularity.

❑

Summary Report of the Conference (Re-Union)

—*Amb. Manju Seth*

ARSP has been undertaking a wide range of activities in order to engage with and expand its outreach to Indian diaspora worldwide. However, contacts and interaction with the Francophone diaspora has been quite limited.

To address this lacuna, ARSP, for the first time, organised a one-day workshop in Reunion Island on 7th July 2018, in consultation with, and the support of the Consul General (CG) of India in Reunion Island, Mr. Babu Paul.

The workshop was organised at the prestigious MOCA venue with enthusiastic participation by the diaspora as well as by the local administration. At the inaugural session (chaired by the CG), the CG welcomed the holding of this first-ever interaction with the diaspora in Reunion Island, by the ARSP, and hoped that this would go a long way in removing the feeling of neglect in the minds of the diaspora. Amb. Virendra Gupta, in his inaugural remarks, spoke of this first endeavour by ARSP to connect with the Francophone Diaspora, especially with the 2,80,000, strong diaspora of Reunion Island who contribute to the economic, social, cultural and political life of Reunion Island, adding that this interaction would lead to creating inter-linkages for mutual benefit and enhance people-to-people contacts. The Mayor of the capital city of St.

Summary Report of the Conference (Re-Union) 201

Denis, Mr. Gilbert Annette spoke of the strong cultural connect with India and that Tamil, Hindi and Gujarati classes had been started in schools as also Yoga lessons.

Mr. Jean Hughes Ratenon, Hon'ble Member of Parliament, in his keynote remarks welcomed and appreciated this first-ever visit by a delegation from India adding that the Reunnionaise Indian diaspora has for long kept India in their hearts; they looked to India for issue of OCI cards and hoped that both the Indian and French governments would resolve the matter as the records were destroyed; he said he would take up the matter with the French government in Paris. Ms. Lynda Lee Mow Sim, Vice President of the Regional Council, spoke of the contribution of the diaspora to the vibrant culture of Reunion Island which had a mix of diaspora from amongst others, Africa and China, and the intermixing had led to a Creole culture, but with Indian culture as the predominant one. All three expressed appreciation for this initiative by ARSP and hoped that this would mark the beginning of many more such interactions.

The afternoon session workshop was chaired by Amb. Manju Seth and was on the combined themes of:

1. Diaspora Connect: Enhancement of cultural and educational linkages between India and Reunion Island; and

2. Promotion of Tourism between India and Reunion Island.

In her opening remarks, Amb. Manju Seth spoke of the importance of this outreach report by ARSP to interact with, and listen to, the Francophone diaspora in Reunion Island with a view to better understand their concerns and expectations and enhance two-way dialogues. The Indian delegation made brief interventions: Mr. Shyam Parande, SG, ARSP, said that greater two-way interaction between India and Reunion was needed, adding that it was interesting to observe that the Reunion people had adopted both Indian values and ethos and elements of France in their lifestyles, clothes

202 *Diaspora and Nation-Building*

and cuisine. Amb. Dayakar, Sr VP of ARSP, highlighted the emphasis given by Indian diaspora to culture and education, which helped them to transform their lives and move from the margins to mainstream life in their host countries adding that multi-culturalism and tolerance are inherent in Indians. Prof. Ajay Dubey of JNU, stated that Reunionnaise diaspora constituted 5% of all Indian Diaspora and despite French policy of integration, they are the only Francophone Diaspora to retain Indian culture and customs while being French in their lifestyles; He made three proposals for mutual benefit: (i) Reunion is like Europe in Africa and could be a gateway for India to connect with Francophone Africa; (ii) MOUs have been signed for Educational exchanges, including between JNU & Reunion University, but flow of students/Professors low due to visa and language issues and recognition of degrees which need to be addressed; (iii) huge potential of Heritage tourism which needs to be tapped.

From the Reunion side, Mr. Jean Regis Ramasamy, historian/journalist proposed that Reunion could be a gateway for India to Europe; it could help connect with the Francophone Indian diaspora in the Caribbean; he would like an Indian Institute to be set up in Reunion on the lines of the Confucius Institute; Reunion needs help and expertise from India in some fields like urban violence, etc. Dr. Selvam Chanemougame, president of the Tamij Sangam, welcomed the visit of the largest ever Indian delegation to Reunion Island stating that they had waited for 30 years for India to use and leverage their strengths but both India and Paris had ignored Reunion, but a beginning has been made now; he also stressed on the need for mutual recognition of degrees. Ms. Sabine Paulic Armoudom, President of ARRCC, briefly outlined three projects that were being pursued and requested support for their implementation, viz. (i) recognition of classical Indian Dance degrees by the French Government (Indian dance is taught at the conservatory, but the teachers's

Summary Report of the Conference (Re-Union) 203

degree from India is not recognised at par with the degrees for western dances); (ii) Training in Yoga at three levels needed and recognition request required to be made to the French government and by AYUSH of the Centre and certificates issued by ARRCC; (iii) support requested for the visit of a CHU (Centre Hospitalier Universitaire, Reunion) delegation to India to discuss with Ministry of AYUSH for signing an MOU to introduce Ayurveda as alternative medicine therapy in CHU and conduct joint research; and to get Ayurveda experts to work in Reunion Island. Ms. Rabia Badat, V.P. of Association Musalman, requested that business visas be facilitated and given for longer periods to enable frequent and easy business travel to India; Students from Reunion could be facilitated to study in the Indian Engineering colleges and more cultural troupes need to perform in Reunion Island.

Mr. Utchanah, President, GOPIO International, made a number of suggestions, viz., OCI cards to be given more liberally for Francophone countries; separate group for KIP from Francophone countries; Francophone session in PBD 2019; EAM could come to Reunion Island from Mauritius when she comes for the Hindi Conference; Ayush Ministry to set up Ayurveda Centres/hospitals in PIO countries including Reunion Island; Indian Universities toast up campuses abroad; more cultural troupes, including Tamil, Hindi, Gujarati, every year to be sent from India and Reunion Island could be a wedding destination for Indians. Prof. R.K. Bhatia, Chairman, PIOCCI, conveyed that PIOCCI would facilitate businessmen to come to India and also promote two way tourism. Mr. Mukesh Aggarwal stated that faculty exchanges between the Universities would be beneficial; Ms. Sarita Budhoo from Mauritius said that today the cultural connect was strong and difficulties faced by the first migrants had been overcome; pioneering work had been done by Mr. Paul Canuguy and Yogesh Bonne in trying to trace roots. Mr. Henri Amogon-Poule, President GOPIO Reunion, stressed that rejuvenating

204   *Diaspora and Nation-Building*

existing links was important; requested support for signing an MOU for twinning between Puducherry and St. Pierre and Karaikal with another city.

In the open house session, interventions were made by Mr. Joel Naraynin, CEO, Akoya Hotel, hoped that Indians would give a boost to ecotourism and visit Reunion Island; Dr. Guy Pignolet, Scientific Advisor, suggested that autobiography of former president, Abdul Kalam, could be distributed to schools in Reunion Island and proposed cooperation in study of outer space; Mr. Tartrist, of Reunion University, stated that the University would like to set up an India Institute on similar lines as the Confucius Institute, funded by both sides; under the EU's Erasmus programme, funding of 1 Million Euros is available and any problems would be resolved with the assistance of the Prefet of Reunion Island; Mr. Yogesh Bonne, President, ACTIR, said that the problem of finding roots of the Francophone diaspora could be resolved and OCI cards issued if access to archives in India (in Chennai and Kolkata) could be facilitated; Prof. Sheetal Sharma, JNU, stated that the existing channels should be utilised for student and faculty exchanges, including GIAN; Prof. Atanu Mohapatra proposed direct links in cultural, technological, design and fashion fields; Mr. Jean Regis Ramasamy suggested joint research in education and culture and historical research, access to information on trade fairs in India, and possibly Heritage tours; Mr. Armoudom, President France-India group, said the main problem of OCI and visas for Reunion people needed to be resolved at the earliest; Dr. Lena Armoudom, President, Committee for indentured Indian labour, suggested that India use and leverage its diaspora as Reunion is essentially Europe in the Indian Ocean; Mr. Ludovic, President Chinmaya Mission, said that an Institute for Indian Ocean studies should be set up ; an IIM and IIT campus can be set up in Reunion Island and can be utilised to help students from Francophone Africa; he

Summary Report of the Conference (Re-Union) 205

suggested setting up a Chamber or Business Club in Reunion to export to the African markets.

In his concluding remarks, Amb. Anup Mudgal, while appreciating the frank interaction and the many suggestions made, said that the ARSP would cull out the doable core issues and take these up and forward concrete proposals with outcomes, to the government and other agencies for implementation.

Disclaimer: *"The opinions and views expressed in this compilation are those of the authors. Only those articles which were forwarded to ARSP by the participants at the conference have been included in this publication".*

□

About the Contributors/Authors

H.E. Mr. Paramasivum Pillay Vyapoory, *GOSK*
The Acting President of the Republic of Mauritius

The Rt. Hon. Sir Anerood Jugnauth, GCSK, KCMG, QC
Minister Mentor, Minister of Defence, Minister for Rodrigues, Republic of Mauritius

Hon. Mr. Anil Kumarsingh Gayan
Minister of Tourism of the Republic of Mauritius

Hon. Mr. Prithvirajsing Roopum
Minister of Culture of the Republic of Mauritius

Mr. Dharam Yash Deo Dhuny
Chairman, Aapravasi Ghat Trust Fund, Port Louis, Mauritius

Amb. Virendra Gupta
President, Antar Rashtriya Sahayog Parishad, Retired Indian Foreign Service officer

Shri. Shyam Parande
Secretary General, Antar Rashtriya Sahayog Parishad

Mrs. Sooryakanti Nirsimloo-Gayan
Director, Mahatma Gandhi Institute and Rabindranath Tagore Institute, Mauritius

About the Contributors/Authors

Amb. Anup K. Mudgal
Chairman, Diaspora Committee, Antar Rashtriya Sahayog Parishad, Retired Indian Foreign Service officer

Shri Rajesh Gogna
Secretary General, Human Rights Defence International

Amb. Manju Seth
Retired Indian Foreign Service officer

Dr. Amba Pande
Assistant Professor, School of International Studies, Jawaharlal Nehru University, New Delhi

Dr. Atanu Mohapatra
Associate Professor & Chairperson in Centre for Studies and Research in Diaspora, Central University of Gujarat, Gandhinagar

Mr. Jayganesh Dawosing
Lecturer, Head department of Bhojpuri, Mahatama Gandhi Institute, Mauritius

Dr. Jean Regis Ramsamy
Historian, Indian Diaspora Council (IDC), delegate, Reunion

Mr. Jwala Rambarran
Former Governor of Central Bank, Trinidad & Tobago

Mrs. Kiran Jankee
Research Officer, Aapravasi Ghat Trust Fund, Mauritius

Dr. Sarita Boodhoo
Chairperson of the Bhojpuri Speaking Union, Mauritius

Dr. Sheetal Sharma
Assistant Professor, School of International Studies, Jawaharlal Nehru University, New Delhi

Dr. Sheilana Devi Ramdoo
Lecturer/School of Performing Arts, Mahatma Gandhi Institute, Mauritius

Mr. Surujdeo Mangaroo
Public Relations officer of the National Council of Indian Culture (NCIC), Trinidad & Tobago

Mrs. Zareen Nishaat Beebeejaun
Lecturer, Mahatma Gandhi Institute, Mauritius

□□□

Printed in the USA
CPSIA information can be obtained
at www.ICGtesting.com
LVHW041147041023
760081LV00009B/215/J